# MISSING
## *Christmas*

My Life in the Depression and World War II

A gift to

_____

from

_____

D0814260

_____

# MISSING *Christmas*

## My Life in the Depression and World War II

# MISSING *Christmas*

## My Life in the Depression and World War II

By
Jack D. Ellis

**JSF**
**JESSE STUART**
**FOUNDATION**

ISBN: 1-931672-67-9


Book Design by

Designs
on You!

Suzanna & Anthony Stephens
www.designs-on-you.net



Published by

Jesse Stuart Foundation
1645 Winchester Avenue
Ashland, Kentucky 41101
(606) 326-1667
JSFBOOKS.com

# TABLE OF CONTENTS

# DEDICATION

This book is dedicated to my many courageous comrades in the 32nd Troop-Carrier Squadron in WWII—and to those brave airborne troops delivered to their "drop zone." Also, to those civilians on the home-front who sacrificed greatly to "keep-em-flying."

O thus be it ever when free men shall stand
Between their loved home and wars desolation!
…Then conquer we must, when our cause it is just!
And this be our motto "In God is our trust."
And the Star-Spangled Banner in triumph shall wave,
O'er the land of the free and the home of the brave!

*Star Spangled Banner* (3rd verse)

# ACKNOWLEDGMENTS

There have been so many individuals and institutions instrumental in preparing this book it is impossible to name them all. However, at the risk of missing some, I want to gratefully acknowledge many of those who have made special contributions.

First, I am extremely grateful for the encouragement and influence of the late Dr. Thomas D. Clark, Kentucky's own "Mr. History," and "History Laureate for Life." We served together on the Kentucky Library and Archives Commission for 34 years, and he graciously wrote introductions to two of my previous books. His influence continues in this book.

Secondly, my deep appreciation goes to all of those members of the late, great 32nd Troop Carrier Squadron of WWII. In addition, I offer a special thanks to former pilot Donald Van Reken for his scholarly book, *History of the 32nd Troop Carrier Squadron 1942 - 1945*, and for permitting me to use some of his materials. Also, other squadron members including former pilots Harley Shotliff and David Rosengrant, who helped collect and preserve the squadron's precious archives, before they were turned over to me to organize and send to Dover Air Force Base in Delaware. Also, my sincere appreciation to Fred Wagner, President of the 32nd T.C.S. (and his dear wife Paddee), who kept the squadron reunions going for many years following WWII. It was in existence from 1976 to 2009. The last reunion was held in 2008, and only four squadron members were able to attend.

I offer a very special thanks to Mrs. Ruth Crisp Robinson who patiently typed and re-typed this manuscript and stored it on a computer disk and to Elsie Pritchard, Dean of Libraries at Morehead State University, and her capable staff, who were extremely helpful in researching this book.

My deep appreciation goes to Donna Baker, Special Collections Librarian at MSU, who diligently scanned the photos onto a computer disk. Thanks also go to Jeff Fannin and his capable staff at the Good Shepherd Printing Services who professionally prepared the photos for scanning.

A special thanks to Dr. C. Nelson Grote, President Emeritus of Morehead State University, and Helen Williams, Librarian at the Rowan County Public Library, who read portions of the manuscript and made many valuable suggestions. As a life-long librarian who just recently received a 55-year pin of continuous membership in the American Library Association, I can appreciate the difficult mechanics of publishing a book; therefore, I wish to express my appreciation to Dr. James M. Gifford and Brett Nance at the Jesse Stuart Foundation for their professional guidance throughout this process.

Last, but by no means least, I want to publicly thank Janis Ruth Caudill Ellis, the love of my life for more than three score years. She patiently put up with me during my grouchy time when the words just would not flow. She also helped to "fine tune" and edit multiple editions of this manuscript.

#  FOREWORD

"All gave some, and some gave all" are the words from that stirring patriotic song by Kentucky's own Billy Ray Cyrus. The book you are holding in your hand is about one of the millions who "gave some" during World War II. Another Kentucky native, Abraham Lincoln, is quoted as saying, "God must have loved the poor people because he made so many of them." I often thought during WWII that God must have loved the American GIs because he made so many of them. At this writing, these men are dying at the rate of more than 1,000 per day and each of these men had a story to tell.

This is my story. I am one of those almost sixteen million soldiers who answered the country's call during WWII and one of less than two million still alive at this time. My story is **not** a story of bravery under fire, nor **heroism** in the line of duty. It is an account of the everyday life of one GI who grew up in the depression years, attended high school during the early years of The War, and enlisted in the military at the age of 17 at the height of that conflict. Therefore, this book relates much of what was happening in "small town America" before the war, as well as what was happening on the home front during the early years of WWII.

Reams have been written about World War II, and many million more words will be written by future historians in an attempt to explain what happened during that conflict and how it affected—

and still affects—millions of people around the world. This book is an attempt to personalize how it affected one small Appalachian community, one family and one soldier who served in that conflict.

Those of us who are veterans of WWII were also veterans of the Great Depression. Because of when we were born, those who were old enough to serve in WWII grew up in a time of great economic turmoil and tribulation in our land. Throughout our childhood we were sometimes hungry, often cold and usually poorly clad, facing an uncertain future. Early in life we learned the meaning of sacrifice by doing without what many would call the "basic necessities of life." I lived without electricity during most of my childhood, and had no indoor plumbing until I was a senior in high school. About the only bright spot in those dull Depression years was the Christmas season. Christmas time was bright not because of gifts we received, because those were few and far between. But it was a joyous time of hope in Christ, singing Christmas carols, hearing church bells ringing, and having family time together.

In looking back through the telescope of time at those years of sacrifice during the Great Depression, it seems those were years of preparing the nation for WWII. During the Depression years, families lost their homes, many times moving back in with grandparents. Many men left home to join the Civilian Conservation Corp (CCC), a quasi military group under the direction of the War Department. These men lived in a military style camp and sent most of their pay home to support their family. Service in the CCC Camp helped prepare them for military service when they sent their allotment check home to their family. Also, families being separated during the depression helped prepare families for the separation which would come during WWII.

The WWII generation has been called "The Greatest Generation" by news anchor Tom Brokaw. Whether we were the "greatest generation," or not, will be determined by future historians. But we were an unselfish generation who asked for very little and seldom complained. When our nation needed men and women as WWII exploded, we responded in overwhelming numbers. We left home, hearth, education and career to answer the call when the country we loved was bombed into war. We never once stopped to consider our own future. Before that war ended, some 16 million had taken the sacred oath to "Protect and defend the constitution of the United States of America against all enemies, both foreign and domestic, so help us God." After taking that oath, we were in for the duration of the war plus six months. Four hundred thousand men did not return—they gave their all and were the **true heroes of WWII**. Our nation and the lives of those of us who did return were changed forever.

# INTRODUCTION

Following World War I, our nation entered a decade of national prosperity. Businesses flourished, and the standard of living rose. Jobs were plentiful and Americans were better fed, clothed, and housed than they had ever been before. During the "Golden Twenties," Americans also experienced profound changes in societal and moral values. Our nation became more urban and industrial, and the protestant ethic was replaced, in many places, by a permissive society characterized by a greater consumption of alcohol and a more liberal attitude toward premarital sex.

However, the prosperity of the "roaring twenties" did not filter down to the rural poor of Appalachia. When Jack Ellis was born to Lon and Dot Ellis in 1927, the family lived near Morehead, Kentucky in a "dilapidated, leaky, rat-infested house with no screens on the windows and one room that had a dirt floor." By the time Jack entered grade school, America was mired in the Great Depression. During the 30s, his father was employed by the Civilian Conservation Corp for several years, but his mother became discouraged and depressed after losing her teaching position in the Rowan County schools.

In 1940, Jack began his freshman year in high school. The following year, when he was within one month of his fifteenth birthday, the Japanese bombed Pearl Harbor, and American life changed dramatically for Jack and the young men and women of his generation, many of whom served for the duration of the war. It was one of the darkest and most painful periods of American history.

On battlefields across the world—at Corregidor, Bastogne, Bataan, and thousands of other death sites—young Americans felt especially alone at Christmas. It was a desperate time for our nation, for our soldiers, and for millions of families who were separated from their sons and daughters during five Christmas seasons.

Jack Ellis did not see himself as a hero, but just another GI doing his best to serve and survive. He missed three Christmases at home during World War II. Like millions of fellow GIs, the song *I'll Be Home for Christmas* had special meaning; the last two lines were

> I'll be home for Christmas,
> If only in my dreams.

The following memoir details Ellis's experiences during the depression and World War II. This book is more than just a testimony to one man's service. It honors every man and woman who served our country during World War II. They were an extraordinary generation. They won the war, enforced the peace, and proudly led our country through the second half of the twentieth century. Sixteen million served in the armed forces, and millions more supported them at home. Through military service, the "greatest generation" learned lessons of teamwork, initiative, sacrifice, and self discipline. They came home trained and experienced, put the horrors of war behind them, and built an even greater nation.

Today, the World War II generation is marching into the pages of history. We are losing thousands of them every day. As a token of our gratitude to and respect for Jack Ellis and every member of America's greatest generation, the Jesse Stuart Foundation is proud to publish this book.

Members of the Greatest Generation, we salute you!

—*James M. Gifford*
*September 2010*

# CHAPTER I

## Depression Christmas: Prelude to War

"Be steadfast knowing ye are partakers of suffering" (II Cor. 1:7)

It has been said that "peace is merely a resting period between wars." Those periods of peace are, many times, spent preparing for war. The Great Depression of the 1930s proved to be a period preparing our nation and our citizens for WWII. It was a time of shortages of food and the basic necessities of life. The suffering and sacrifices of our people during the Great Depression prepared us as a people for the shortages, separation, suffering, and sacrifices that we would face during WWII.

The Great Depression taught us patience in waiting for something to happen. It taught us as a people to persevere during hunger, cold, and with the barest of necessities for daily living. It taught us to "make do" with what we had and make it work for what we needed. That helped prepare us as a people for rationing and shortages during WWII.

Much has been written about the Great Depression. It is not the kind of "depression" one has when the doctor writes you a prescription for a mood-enhancing drug. That kind of "depression" is defined in the dictionary as a "psychotic disorder marked by feelings of sadness, dejection, inactivity, and lowering of vitality." However, that is a good definition of how millions of Americans felt in the 1930s following the collapse of the stock market and this nation's economy. But there were no mood enhancing drugs for those who lived through those trying times.

The economic calamity called the "Great Depression" that struck this nation in the late 1920s and the 1930s has usually been viewed from a national perspective, just as WWII is usually viewed from an international perspective. Statistics are quoted in the billions of dollars and millions of people. However, with that perspective, one can lose sight of the individual and personal suffering and sacrifices during that tragic time in our nation's history.

With no jobs, men loafed in front of the local A&P Store. *Photo: National Archives*

What follows is an attempt to focus on a single Appalachian County in the heartland of America. It is an attempt to personalize some of the events of the Great Depression. Rowan County, with a population of 12,000, is located in the eastern section of Kentucky. It could be considered typical of the Appalachian section of America. Its county seat is Morehead, the site of Morehead State College (now Morehead State University).

It has been said that the definition of a recession is when your neighbor is broke and out of a job, while a depression is when you're broke and unemployed. When you and your neighbor are both broke and unemployed, it is really bad. The terrible stock market crash in 1929 triggered what was to become known as the "Great Depression." Soon many people in Morehead and Rowan County were broke and out of work. Although Morehead was the location of a state college, Rowan County was basically an agricultural county and the Great Depression brought poverty to the county. Students could not afford to go to college, and many people were hungry and cold with little hope for the future.

There were two factories in Rowan County during the depression years: the Lee-Clay Tile Factory in Clearfield and the Kentucky Fire Brick Company at Haldeman. They both survived by reducing hours and by working about two days a week. They even alternated work days with their employees and some only were able to work one day a week. But the 25 cents per hour they made, and their own small farms and gardens enabled many to eke out an existence, until the government "alphabet agencies" began to put people back to worthwhile work in their communities.

## THE DEPRESSION BRINGS "DEPRESSION"

The Great Depression not only brought terrible economic

conditions to this nation, but it also brought great personal "depression" as well as tragedy and suffering to many individuals and families.

Growing up during the Great Depression left me with bleak, sad, and traumatic memories of living in a dirty, dilapidated, leaky, four-room, rat infested house with no screens on the windows and one room with a dirt floor. That room had no inside wallboard or ceiling covering of any kind. The rafters and wall studs were all exposed and as I played with my tiny toy truck amid the mounds of dirt, I could see to the top underside of the roof. But one memory of that room remains seared into my psyche even to this day.

I was about seven- or eight-years old and my mother had not yet been hired as a teacher that year. Dad was a member of the Civiian Conservation Corps (CCC) but could live at home. One Saturday morning my mother and dad were arguing. My mother insisted that my dad take me up to my grandfather's house about two miles away and leave me with my grandparents for the weekend. My dad did not want to do that, but he finally agreed.

My grandparents lived farther up in the Licking Valley, and we walked the two miles to their house but found it empty. A neighbor said they had gone across the river to visit family for the weekend. So my dad and I began our walk back home.

When we entered the house it was strangely silent. After looking in all the rooms and around the house, we went into the room with the dirt floor again, and, with me right behind him, Dad opened the closet door which had no ceiling. There was my mother, with a noose around her neck with the rope tied around the rafter, still struggling for breath. There was a turned over chair beneath her feet.

Dad yelled, "Dot!"

I cried, "Mom!"

Dad quickly lifted her up in his arms to slacken the rope as he loosened the noose around her neck. He carried her out of the room with the dirt floor and placed her on the old couch which was my bed at night. He slapped her face lightly and lifted her back firmly. Finally she was aroused enough to see me and hear me crying. Of course she thought I was gone for the weekend and she had no intention for me to see what was happening.

But I did.

After she was able to get up and walk around, she sat me down on the old couch and said to me in no uncertain terms, "Son, don't you ever tell anybody about this as long as I live. If you do, Mom will not be able to teach school." I didn't tell and she taught school 30 years in Kentucky and 10 years in Florida. She lived to the ripe old age of 90 and was one of the most positive people in the world, She was an encourager, Sunday School teacher, and letter writer all of her life. She was still tutoring children the last year of her

Dot Ellis

life. She loved the Lord with all her heart, soul, and body, and her neighbors as herself. She left a rich legacy of four grandchildren and 11 great-grandchildren.

However, the trauma of her attempted suicide remains with me today. I will always believe that God had His hand in that event. By my returning unexpectedly with my dad, and, as terrible as it was, maybe my being there gave her the desire to continue her life. It was a full and wonderful life.

I never spoke of the event to anyone, even to my wife of 60 years until several years after my mother's death. I include it here to personalize the depression and also to let people know that nothing is ever as bad as it seems. This personal story is told as a tribute to my mother who spent the last 65 years of her life helping others and living life to the fullest.

## DROUGHT AND DEPRESSION DEVASTATE ECONOMY

Because Rowan was basically an agricultural economy, the Great Depression that hit the nation as a result of the stock market crash of 1929 did not immediately affect the local economy. But Rowan County's farmers did suffer financially from the devastating drought that hit this region in 1930. In the years of 1929 and 1930, my father planted 100 acres of corn each year on my grandfather's farm. He did not harvest one ear of corn either year because of a flood on the Licking River the first year and a terrible drought the next year. That drought not only affected the farmers, but Morehead's water supply. There was an extreme water shortage that resulted in water being shipped into Morehead via the C&O and Morehead and North Fork Railroads.

The year of the drought, with practically no city water, residents had to depend on a few private wells. The water that was shipped

The Kentucky Fire Brick Company at Haldeman continued part-time during the Depression. *Photo: Becker Family*

into Morehead via the railroad was stored in a large tank in the middle of town. Residents would bring their buckets there or to a neighbor's well for their water. Lindsay Caudill, who would many years later become my father-in-law, had a well on his property on East Second Street that never did go dry. He provided water to many neighbors whose wells had gone dry during that period. That was the true spirit of neighbor helping neighbor in times of natural and economic disasters.

## LOCAL GOVERNMENTS FIRST TO FEEL EFFECTS

In the early 1930s, Farmers, Kentucky, formerly a booming sawmill town, was one of the first communities in Rowan County to feel the effects of the depression.

Records show that the town trustees, in one of their first cost-cutting measures, refused to accept their $5 per month salary. Next,

Flooded farms were common during the Depression years.

they cut the city marshal's salary to $10 per month before reducing his salary to zero. The tiny town of Farmers' budget shortfall resulted in the former city trustees being charged with malfeasance because they had over-estimated the tax revenue. However, those charges were quickly dismissed because it was determined that the drought and the depression had caused the budget shortfall.

By 1934, the effects of the Depression became more widespread and soon affected every area of government services. The County Board of Education, facing a critical budget shortfall, reduced Superintendent Roy Cornette's salary from $175 per month to $100. (My mother's teacher's salary was reduced to $40 per month.) It caused quite a family conflict when board member, Jesse Boggess, Roy Cornette's brother-in-law and school board member, made the motion to reduce the Superintendent's salary. Also that year, the Board abolished the janitor's job in the Haldeman High School

Crowded one room school at Mt. Hope, Kentucky, 1930s. Dot Ellis, teacher.

1. Denmel Sweeney
2. Liddy Ramey
3. Jr Johnson
4. Delbert Johnson,
5. Gene Cornett
6. Theodore Ellington
7. Jack Staton
8. Ruth Staton
9. Maxine Foster
10. Norma Perry
11. Vernie Middleton
12. Hester Tackett
13. Wilma Staton
14. Jewell Sweeney
15. Deloris Perry
16. Alvin Staton
17. Phylliss Mckinney
18. Olive Ramey
19. Icelene Sweeney
20. Anna Brown
21. Ray Ellington
22. Bronson hayes
23. Lon Gibbs
24. Lylburn Johnson
25. Dot Ellis (Teacher
26. Joyce Mckinney
27. Labe Jr Mckinney
28. Gaddis Jr
29. Earl Ramey
30. Bobby Cornette
30 Bobby Cornette
31. ?
32. Mervil Charles or Hayward Johnson
33. Alfred Gibbs
34. Arley Gibbs
35. Aubry Lewis or Ed Sweeney
36. Delora Perry
37. Ester Peyton
38. Pauline Mckinney
39. Edith Tackett

and required teachers to keep the building clean. Senior teachers at Haldeman and Morehead High School were required to serve as assistant principals without pay. Fewer teachers were hired that year and those that were employed were required to take larger class loads for their $40 per month for nine months' salary. Classes were crowded with 50 - 60 in a class.

There were months the school board could not make their payroll and teachers had to wait for weeks for their checks. Fortunately, local teachers could "discount" their checks by signing them over to the bank, and then they would receive the cash immediately by paying a $1 check cashing fee. In today's economy, those check discount places think they are doing something new. But it certainly is a sign of a depressed economy when those discount check stores flourish.

The Rowan Fiscal Court attempted to cut the cost of county government through reduction of services and belt tightening procedures. Since there was no central county garage, county employees were taking equipment home with them. As a result, it was discovered that thousands of tax dollars had been spent the past few years for road graders and scrapers, and some of the equipment could not even be found. Some former employees even claimed ownership of road equipment that was bought and paid for by county taxes. Also, county equipment was often used on private property. It could be said that one good thing to come out of the Great Depression was greater accountability by local government.

## PEOPLE LOSE JOBS—GO HUNGRY

The Great Depression precipitated a "catch 22" downward spiral in the economy. It made a bad situation even worse because with fewer people employed there was less money to spend. Less spending resulted in fewer sales. Fewer sales resulted in fewer employees, causing a vicious downward economic cycle. That was before income tax, sales tax, occupational tax and many other specific taxing entities, e.g., Library and Health Department taxes. A depressed economy in today's world would be even more devastating to government services. Many land owners lost their land because they could not pay their taxes. This writer's father did not own any property during that era, but my grandfather had to mortgage his farm every year to pay the taxes. As the economy spiraled downward during the early 1930s, local businesses began to feel the effects. Most businesses were forced to retrench in staff and salaries. The owner of the Red Rose Dairy where my father worked had to let him go in order to give a job to his brother. With no unemployment insurance, government

Sorghum provided a sweet treat for children.

support or jobs, millions of people in this nation were unemployed and begging for work. They were willing to do any kind of work.

People in Eastern Kentucky were too proud to beg, but not too proud to steal or make moonshine. As the Great Depression deepened, this writer can recall, many hypothetical discussions revolved around the question, "if your family was starving would you steal?" Since tobacco was not bringing enough to pay to get it to market, some families made molasses, and other families made moonshine as cash crops during the Great Depression.

## FAMILIES MOVED BACK TOGETHER

It was a time when young married couples with children moved back in with parents and grandparents. When my dad lost his job at

Making sorghum brought cash during lean years. (George Caudill brought his own buckets.)

the dairy, we had to move back to the farm with my grandparents. My wife, Janis Caudill, says that when her dad lost his job on the C&O Railroad, they also had to move back in with her grandparents. Not only did families help families, neighbors helped neighbors during the era of the Great Depression. Many neighbors literally helped keep some of their neighbors alive during that era.

In the year 2000, I visited an elderly gentleman in the hospital. When he found out that my grandfather was the John Ellis who once owned a farm along the Licking River Valley, he told me with tears in his eyes, "Our family would have starved to death during the Depression if it had not been for your grandfather. He provided us with meat, milk, fruit and vegetables, and, on occasion, a job to buy sugar and salt." That was true of many, many families during that era. At first, it was a time that there was no government help, only families helping families and neighbors helping neighbors. The Great Depression brought families and neighbors together in a common battle of survival during the toughest economic times this nation ever faced.

The factory towns of Haldeman and Clearfield were much better off than other areas of Rowan County. Even though those brick and tile factories operated on a very limited basis, they still managed to provide one or two days work each week for many men. Many men walked miles to work those one or two days a week, often leaving home with their lanterns before daylight and returning home after dark. But they had to have those one or two days work; and even with their own small farms and gardens, they were barely able to get by.

## DEPRESSION GHOSTS OF CHRISTMAS PAST

Deep within the inner recesses of our minds are special memories we hold dear. Many of these memories revolve around holidays, especially Christmas holidays. One might think that growing up in the era of the Great Depression, there would be few happy memories. However, we seem to forget the hard times, and tend to remember the happy times, especially those memorable "ghosts" of Christmas past.

One "Ghost of Christmas Past" many Rowan Countians hold dear in their heart is the Haldeman community Christmas. Owner L.P. Haldeman and the employees of the Haldeman Fire Brick Company generously sponsored the program each year. It was one of the outstanding holiday events in Rowan County during those otherwise drab depression years of the 1930s. There were bands, school programs, concerts in the new high school auditorium, and, of course, gifts were distributed to the children. Music was provided by the 25-member band from the new Haldeman Consolidated School.

Everyone in Haldeman and in that area of Rowan County looked

Firebrick workers' homes in Haldeman, Kentucky. *Photo: Becker Family*

forward every year to the annual Holiday Community Christmas Program. Each year during the 1930s, a large tree was brought into the little village where the decorations were waiting to be hung on the tree by the children. It was decorated by children and adults, and, on Christmas Eve, all the wide-eyed children gathered around the beautifully decorated tree where they breathlessly waited for Jolly Old St. Nicholas to arrive with presents for all. He never disappointed them and the lives of the children growing up in Rowan County during the bleak 1930s were brightened every year when Santa Claus arrived in Haldeman.

The Haldeman Christmas program was a major event in the lives of the people in that community and the entire county. I was never invited to those Haldeman programs, but many people from other areas of Rowan County were invited to attend and enjoy that annual event. Those 1930s days of the community Christmas

These boys brought their Christmas cap pistols to school to "play war," 1937. L to R: Meredith Mynhier, Jack Ellis, unidentified, unidentified, Ernest Reynolds, and Harve Manning, Jr. All served in WWII.

programs in Haldeman are one of the Merry Christmas memories of many Rowan Countians because of the joy and happiness it brought into their lives.

Another bright Christmas memory in an otherwise dark depression era was the annual free movie at the Cozy Theater in Morehead. The movie was free to all of the children of Morehead and Rowan County. (I well remember that special memory of Christmas.) It was sponsored by theater owners Hartley Battson and H.C. Willet. Every year the small theater was crowded with noisy happy excited children. Many who attended had never before seen a movie and were doubly excited. Most years the Cozy Theater was so crowded that two showings were necessary to accommodate the crowd.

Although it was not required, Mr. Battson and Mr. Willet, in the true spirit of Christmas, suggested that each child bring a Christmas gift and drop into a large barrel in the lobby. Practically every child brought a gift and usually large barrels of gifts were collected and turned over to the local women's club. The Red Cross then distributed those gifts to the many children in the county who might not otherwise receive a gift. *Rowan County News* editor, Jack Wilson, pointed out how people were helping their neighbors during that Great Depression Christmas. He complimented the people of Morehead for their generous Christmas spirit in the following editorial dated December 19, 1932:

### "Morehead in the Christmas Spirit"

Speaking of the spirit of Christmas, the spirit of giving, the spirit of carrying joy and gladness into the lives of those unfortunate children who, through no fault of their own are unable to enjoy the season, the people of Morehead have a right to be proud of themselves for the remarkable gift barrels they filled at the Cozy Theater on Monday evening. The announcement was made through the columns of this paper, that the management of the Cozy was giving their annual free show on that evening and requesting that all who attended the show, bring with them some little package, some old toy or article of clothing that would serve to make happy the heart of a child, who otherwise might not be able to enjoy Christmas. Remember Christmas is a time of giving as well as receiving, and it is more blessed to give than to receive.

The response was truly wonderful. Instead of a small

barrel of gifts, there was not only a large barrel full, but a large box full as well. Every gift was wrapped in Christmas paper and tied with Christmas ribbon, thus carrying out in detail the thought that makes Christmas the happy season it is. And not all the gifts were old. Many of the great hearted had gone to the stores and purchased gifts, new toys, new stockings, new clothing.

It was the spirit of old time Christmas that prevailed, a spirit that in the rush and hurry of modern life, and a dreary depression has more or less been forgotten or overlooked. And as such, this Christmas is a Christmas to remember. For if this season has a lesson for anyone, worthy of the learning, it is the lesson of unselfishness and the lesson of charity. And it would seem that Morehead and Rowan County have learned the lesson well.

Whether you brought a gift or received a gift, those free Cozy Christmas Movies remain happy memories to this writer and a "Ghost of Christmas Past" to many Moreheadians.

## ECONOMY SLOWLY IMPROVED

Other ghosts of Christmas Past in Rowan County in 1935 include political, business, and government ghosts. That year many Morehead businesses were predicting improved sales over the past few Christmases. Employment at the Clearfield and Haldeman Factories had improved, and of course, the College provided a sound base to the local economy. Also, over 400 men had been employed

## A Few Gift Suggestions
### At Bishop's
### 1935

#### For Men

Cameras
Lighter
Stropper
Fountain Pens
Card Sets
Smoking Set
Military Sets
Pipes

#### For Women

Powder
Perfumes
Candy
Compacts
Bath Salts
Stationery
Manicure Sets
Brushes

A Depression Christmas gift list, 1935.

under the new Works Program Administration (WPA). Those men were put to work building schools, roads and voting booths. That outlook caused local businesses to increase their inventory and hope for better Christmas sales than during the past years. Their sales did not reach their projection that Christmas, but sales were slowly improving. In 1935 local department stores were pushing feminine gifts such as gloves, bags, silk quilted robes, scarves, umbrellas, lingerie, and collars with cuff sets. Highly advertised men's gifts included corduroy britches, gum boots, and leather boots. Most gifts in the mid-1930s were practical apparel, much needed by both men and women.

## POLITICAL CHRISTMAS

Although the nation was in a depressed economy, certainly politics were very much in evidence during the 1935 Christmas season. Albert B. "Happy" Chandler was inaugurated the new governor of Kentucky. Many from Rowan County were among the 25,000 who attended that event in Frankfort, as the new governor offered hope for the future. William Rogers Clay, Chief Justice of Kentucky, swore in the 37-year-old governor and his Lt. Governor, Keen Johnson, on December 15, 1935. The new governor wasted no time in cleaning house in Frankfort and throughout the state by calling for the resignation of hundreds of people, including some members of the Morehead College Board of Regents who had been appointed by previous Governor Ruby Lafoon. (It was a sad Christmas for those employees fired in the midst of a depression.)

## ELECTION CONTESTED IN ROWAN

There was a contested election in Rowan County during the 1935 Christmas season. In November, C.C. Jennings had defeated J.J. Thomas for County Judge by 81 votes. Mr. Thomas contested the election and hired Mt. Sterling attorney W.C. Hamilton to represent him. Mr. Jennings hired local attorneys Claude Crosthwaite and W.E. Proctor to represent him. The contest did not prevail and Mr. Jennings was declared the winner. Even so, the Kentucky House of Representatives in Frankfort refused to seat Mr. Jennings and he never served his term.

## ECONOMY IMPROVED—WAR CLOUDS APPEAR

"Ghosts of Christmas Past" in Rowan County in 1940 included war worry, savings from Christmas Clubs, tobacco sales, and nativity Christmas pageants. It was the year the economy seemed to improve in Rowan County. That year the Citizens Bank announced they paid more than $5,000 to Christmas club members. Also, that year tobacco farmers received a better price for their tobacco, but the weight was much lighter than the previous year.

In 1940 Rowan County farmers marketed their tobacco early, with most of the crops selling before Christmas. The dry weather retarded the quality in tobacco grading, which resulted in an even greater percentage of the crop going to market at an earlier date. Prices were generally better that year, but less than was expected by most farmers. Some local farmers received near top prices on the markets. Willie Anderson, of Waltz community, received $24.86 a hundred for 2,035 pounds sold December 10. His crop was not all marketed, but the 6,800 pounds sold averaged about $21.00. R.A. Decker, also of the Waltz community, sold 1,172 pounds for an even $24.00 per hundred. Mr. Decker's son sold 294 pounds for $19.50 from the same farm. Others with good sales that year were George Williams and tenant, Othie Springer, of Triplett community. They received $21.68 for 1,398 pounds. Emil Brown of Minor sold his crop of about 1,200 pounds for $21.00. Farmers were generally satisfied with the prices received at the Huntington, West Virginia, market. The improved prices for tobacco that year meant a brighter Christmas in 1940.

A very real "Ghost of Christmas Past" in 1940 was the war clouds that gathered over Britain and much of Europe, involved in an all-out war with Nazi Germany. Also, Japan was fighting with Korea and China. Most people in the U.S. were apprehensive about the U.S. becoming involved in a war. Perhaps because of that war worry, many Moreheadians returned to the church and the basis for Christmas: The birthday of Christ.

## MOREHEAD BIBLICAL CHRISTMAS

In 1940 there was a return to a Biblical Christmas. Christmas that year was a return to a celebration of the Birth of Christ. One example was the Morehead Christian Church's presentation of an extravagant nativity pageant that included a cast of many local Moreheadians. "The Nativity," one of the most beautiful Christmas Pageants was presented in the auditorium of the Christian Church, Sunday evening, December 22, 1941, at 7:30 o'clock.

The Nativity Service was composed entirely of scriptural selections, arranged in dramatic form on the plan of a mystery play, picturing the Bible story of the Nativity and accompanied by Christmas carols. It was a wonderfully unique and impressive service, produced in thousands of churches throughout the nation.

There were four scenes in the pageant as follows: "The Temple"; "The Annunciation"; "The Shepherds"; and the "Nativity." The cast included Mabel Carr as Mary, Walter Carr as Joseph, Frances Peratt as Gabriel, Richard Dougherty as Zacharias, James Reynolds, Talmadge Cline and Thomas Powers as Shepherds. It included Ollie Lyons, Leo Davis Oppenheimer, Robert Hogge as Wise Men, and the Morehead Christian Church Choir under the leadership of L.E. Blair, as the Heavenly Host. Mrs. E.D. Williams and Mrs. A.E. Landolt, both of whom were experienced in play production, directed the Pageant. Mrs. H.L. Wilson assisted in the music.

The service seemed to have a lasting impression on all who saw it.

## FEW CHRISTMAS HOLIDAYS

During the Great Depression all the children in the Rowan County schools had to go to school right up to Christmas Eve. The schools in Rowan County had their Christmas programs on Christmas Eve, December 24. Following their programs, the children were dismissed until December 30th. They were not out of school on New Year's Eve or New Year's Day. That was not only a "Ghost of Christmas Past" for many Rowan County School children, it would be a nightmare for many of today's school children.

In the summer of 1932 with the nation in the throes of the depression, there were eleven million men out of work. Families in Rowan County and throughout this nation were going hungry. Eleven thousand jobless veterans of World War I marched on Washington, DC, demanding a bonus for their military service in the Great War. (Some of that group, called Cox's Army, camped in Rowan County on their way.) But when they arrived, they were met with violence in the nation's capital. Upon arrival in Washington, DC, and acting on orders from President Hoover, General MacArthur and Major Dwight Eisenhower's troops burned their makeshift shanties and ran them out of town.

President Hoover was optimistic about the economy in spite of the financial crises that faced the nation, and Congress soon established the Reconstruction Finance Commission. The R.F.C. announced that loans of 49 million were being processed to help depressed areas throughout the nation. By the end of 1932, $3,440 had trickled down to Rowan County, but failed to make much of an impact. However, help was still a long time coming in the form of President Roosevelt's New Deal and all of the "alphabet agencies."

## NEW PRESIDENT—NEW DEAL—ALPHABET AGENCIES ARRIVE

That fall President Hoover was overwhelmingly rejected by the American people and Franklin D. Roosevelt was elected President. He carried all but six states with his campaign promise to launch a frontal attack on the four horsemen of the Republican leadership: "The horsemen of Destruction, Delay, Deceit and Despair." Roosevelt carried Rowan County 2,844 to 1,622.

Upon taking office, Roosevelt declared "The only thing we have to fear is fear itself," and his first 100 days in office launched his "New Deal." That new deal enacted legislation for a litany of alphabet agencies including the Agricultural Adjust Act (AAA), Civilian Conservation Corps (CCC), Federal Emergency Relief Administration (FERA), Civil Works Administration (CWA), Public Workers Administration (PWA), and Works Progress Administration (WPA). All were established P.D.Q., A.S.A.P. and all profoundly affected this nation and Rowan County, helping to move us out of the Great Depression.

Although the CCC Camp was the first of the New Deal programs in Rowan County, there were many others to make an impact upon the county. The city, county and college had clear ideas of what they needed and soon those ideas began to materialize. The Fiscal court built a county garage on Christy Creek to protect the county equipment. The city soon received funds for a new sewer system and jail. Also, Morehead College built a new sewage system that was vital to their needs which reinforced the city's request for funds.

## FOOD ARRIVES—MEN GO TO WORK—STUDENTS GO TO COLLEGE

In February, 1934, the Federal Emergency Relief Act sent 4,100 pounds of smoked bacon into Rowan County. It was distributed to those hungry in the county through the Fiscal Court. Other FERA activities included building three county roads (Farmers to Sharkey, Open Fork to Haldeman and the Allie Young Highway (now State Route 32 to Flemingsburg). By using a system of rotation, the road work provided 500 men with the dignity of a job and helped provide food for their family. Also, FERA provided workships that allowed 52 Morehead College students an opportunity to continue their education.

# Cox's Army

There has been more than one "Cox's army." The first one featured in American history books was led by Jacob Cox, a Union general who later wrote a two-volume memoir about the Civil War and who was part of General William Sherman's infamous "march to the sea." However, the Cox's army that marched to Washington, D.C., during the Great Depression was led by a Catholic priest. Father James Renshaw Cox who organized one of the most famous demonstrations ever held in Washington, D.C. Father Cox, a former steelworker and taxi driver, had worked his way through college and then attended Catholic seminary. He served as a chaplain in World War I, and after that war, he worked with the poor and homeless in his parish in Pittsburgh. On January 10, 1932, leaving from the steps of St. Patrick's Roman Catholic Church, he got into a red truck that led a convoy of trucks and cars carrying World War I veterans from Pittsburgh to Washington. Because so many millions of people were in desperate situations during the hard times after the 1929 crash of Wall Street, and because the men were war veterans, people along the way generally treated them with respect. Oil magnate (and Secretary of the Treasury) Andrew Mellon told his Gulf Oil stations to give the drivers in the motor cavalcade free gas on their 300-mile route from Pittsburgh to Washington. On the morning of the march, the U.S. Army sent them a breakfast of apples, doughnuts, and coffee from Fort Myers. Reports vary, but somewhere between 10,000 and 17,000 men lined up eight abreast and marched to the Capitol building, where Father Cox read a petition to Congress. The petition asked for a federal works program to give jobs to the unemployed, and it asked for an increase of taxes on gifts and inheritances to help fund public programs. Cox then went to President Hoover's office and read the petition to him. The good will didn't last for their entire visit, and the demonstrators were routed with little respect for their veteran status. Before returning with other marchers to Pittsburgh, Father Cox and some of the other men went to Arlington to lay a wreath at the tomb of the Unknown Soldier. President Hoover's failure to do anything in response to this demonstration—except fire Mellon from his job as Secretary of the Treasurer and have Cox investigated after the march—helped lead to Franklin Roosevelt's victory in the next presidential election.

By mid-year 1934, the Civil Works Administration arrived in Rowan County. Unlike FERA, the CWA workers were actually on the federal payroll. That agency took half of its workers from the relief (poverty) rolls and the other half from the unemployed. Those workers did not have to be at the poverty level. The CWA paid the minimum wage of 25 cents per hour. But most workers were part-time only.

## COURTHOUSE REMODELED WITH NEW DEAL SPENDING

The Rowan CWA office was located in the Courthouse and soon the Fiscal court approved several projects, e.g., remodeling the Courthouse (that was the first remodeling that cut off part of the bell tower.) Other work involved a new county jail and several road building projects. The CWA covered most of the cost. The county paid their portion by renting county trucks at 75 cents per hour and tractors and rock crushers at $1.00 an hour. With little local cost, this made the program politically attractive to the local leaders.

However, President Roosevelt became alarmed and feared the federal relief might become a habit to the political leaders and ordered the program killed as soon as the danger of people starving in cold weather was over. By the end of 1934, $250,000 had been spent in Rowan County on more federal programs. But that was certainly not the end of the New Deal spending in Rowan County. Accounting for the funds in the various alphabet agencies would certainly drive any certified public accountant mad. President Roosevelt had almost unlimited emergency powers and could turn agencies on and off like a water faucet. So many times the agency that began a project wasn't the one that finished it. The creation of the WPA in 1935 is a good case in point.

Morehead State College (MSU) Science Building (now Lappin Hall), a part of "New Deal" construction during Depression.

## PWA AND WPA BRING MANY PROJECTS TO ROWAN COUNTY

The PWA provided $255,000 for a new power plant in Morehead. It also provided for four four-foot high dams on Triplett Creek. It included $440,000 for a science building and a new men's dorm for Morehead State College. These old programs were turned over to the Works Progress Administration (WPA) as new projects. That was not unusual during the years of the Depression. The state was also required to pay a certain percentage of the cost for the College buildings.

In 1935, the WPA established a sewing center in the Rowan Courthouse at a cost of $22,650 with the county paying $180. It taught people sewing as a job opportunity. The city of Morehead received $150,000 to complete the new sewer and jail construction. The Superintendent of Schools received money to hire 25 teachers on a part-time basis to file and prepare the life history of each child in Rowan County.

By the mid-1930s, the alphabet agencies out of Washington, D.C., were beginning to make a positive impact upon Rowan County. Roads and bridges were being built and buildings, power plants, and a new infra-structure were appearing upon the landscape. But above all, people were working again. Not just leaf raking work, but solid construction of institutions that would last–and gradually a light was appearing at the end of the tunnel called the Great Depression. But little did the young men who suffered through the Great Depression realize they would be required to suffer and sacrifice much more during WWII.

## NEW DEAL GOAL: HELP PEOPLE & INSTITUTIONS

President Roosevelt's goal for his New Deal was to help those Americans who were "ill-housed, ill-clad, and ill-nourished." He might have also included "ill-educated" because many of the alphabet agencies, in addition to providing economic assistance to Rowan County, also aided education.

By the mid-1930s, Morehead had been able to pave many city streets, completed a sewer project and built a new jail at a total cost of $150,000. The Superintendent of Schools had employed 25 unemployed teachers to organize the school records, teach agriculture courses, and CCC recruits.

The WPA had constructed school buildings at Haldeman, Farmers and Elliottville out of native bluestone from the Bluestone Quarry. For a time the construction stopped on the Elliottville School until Congressman Fred M. Vinson "greased the political wheels" in Washington and got the additional $16,700 needed to finish the job.

## MEN GIVEN THE DIGNITY OF WORK IN BUILDING A BETTER COMMUNITY

An editorial in the Rowan County News declared "Men will go back to work and the people of this county will have school

Farmers School built of native stone with New Deal (WPA) funds.

buildings that will stand 100 years or more, providing educational opportunities for the children equal to that in more fortunate cities." (The buildings still stand after 80 years, but the educational opportunities have moved into new buildings). The buildings no longer fit the programs.

Other WPA projects which, according to many local people, meant, "we piddle around," included a county garage, $3,423 (county cost $143); 17 native stone voting booths, with one still in use, $11,273 (county cost $2,222); and five farm roads at a cost of $202,550. But the county cost was only $23,700, most of which was paid by

Haldeman School, built of native stone, celebrates Armistice Day. Teacher: Mary Alice Jayne.

Morehead Post Office mural depicts Appalachian life. Artist: Frank Long, 1937.

renting county road machinery. The five road projects employed 650 men. They included 46 semi-skilled workers, 25 skilled workers, and 10 foremen. The remaining were laborers taken from the relief (poverty) rolls. Also, construction of the 17 voting booths employed 18 men, who were selected from the relief rolls.

## CULTURAL PROJECTS ESTABLISHED

The WPA established a number of cultural projects in Rowan County. Those included a library located where McKinney's Shoe Shop was on Carey Avenue. Later it was moved to the basement of the public school on Second Street. A packhorse library was opened in the back of the Caskey Hotel and Dot Ellis was employed as a packhorse librarian for a couple of years. Packhorse librarians were so-called because they delivered books either on horse-back or in cars. The Packhorse Library later burned when the Caskey Hotel burned on July 3, 1939.

Music was not forgotten in the cultural war on poverty. However, Miss Jean Thomas, known locally as "The Traipsin' Woman," and renowned collector of folk songs, directed an old time music concert on the campus of Morehead College. (Morehead College has a rich heritage of folk music reaching back into the 1930s and beyond.) In

1937, nationally famous artist, Frank Long, completed and hung the mural in the new post office at Main Street and Wilson Avenue. (The mural may be seen in the City Government Building today.)

Although the WPA closed its office in Morehead in October, 1938, it was not the end of that program. Following the tragic flash flood that struck Morehead July 4, 1939, claiming 25 lives, the Regional WPA Director in Paintsville sent workers to aid in the cleanup process. Total expenditures in Rowan County through the WPA years totaled $570,000 or nearly 38 percent of Rowan's entire New Deal expenditures. It was estimated that almost three out of four Rowan County men were at one time or another employed under the WPA or other New Deal programs. The jobs were many times only part-time and the pay was 25 cents per hour. Without that 25 cents per hour, however, many would have suffered malnutrition and perhaps even starvation.

## AN ALPHABET AGENCY FOR YOUTH

There seemed to be an alphabet agency for every purpose under the New Deal Program. In order to keep youth in school and out of an already depressed job market, the National Youth Administration, NYA, was created. The Rowan County Youth Council, under the direction of Warren Lappin, administered the program. Another category of the NYA included young men ages 16-25, headed by Buell Hogge They were paid $7 for 44 hours work. The NYA boys (sorry, no girls) built sidewalks at $6 for 50 square feet. They helped build the Board of Education building on the back of the Courthouse lawn. They also built a rock wall on either side of the men's dormitories on the campus of Morehead State College.

In 1935, 75 MSC students held NYA workships. One year later there were 111 in the program and they were paid $7 for 44 hours

Jean Christy (L) and Janis Caudill rest on native stone wall on MSC campus—built by NYA youth.

work. It was enough to pay a student's board at MSC. With the new men's hall and science building on campus, and the NYA workships, President Harvey A. Babb was called "Morehead's New Deal President."

There were dozens of other New Deal agencies created during the Great Depression that funneled money into Rowan County's depressed areas. The World War I veterans received their bonus that brought $142,721 into the local economy. Also by 1937, the Social Security Act brought payments to Rowan County, as well as deductions from paychecks. The first Social Security recipients received just under $10 per month. It is estimated that Uncle Sam paid about two million dollars for the programs used to fight the Great Depression in Rowan County.

## NEW DEAL BROUGHT PERMANENT PROJECTS AND BUILDINGS

With cold hard cash placed in front of them, local city, college, and county administrations began to plan positively and think boldly. Expenditures meant jobs as well as patronage, which was an added incentive to spend. The New Deal brought the county out of the mud with road building, as well as constructing new, modern buildings. Eighty years later, evidence of the New Deal still remains in Rowan County's stone jails, school buildings, and voting booths, as well as roads. Also, bridges, sidewalks, and a fire tower can still be found that were built by the New Deal.

When the CCC camp closed down, School Superintendent Roy Cornette proposed a plan for the abandoned buildings. He wrote Senator A.B. Chandler and Congressman Joe Bates, making a strong case for the buildings by declaring that if the buildings could be obtained by the school system, "Every farm boy in high school in Rowan County would have an opportunity to take vocational

One of 17 stone voting booths built in Rowan County during the Depression era of the early 1930s, but only one remains in use.

agriculture. We also plan to hold special military training classes. Also, farm machinery repair could be carried on more effectively." However, Roy's plan fell on unsympathetic ears and he was unable to keep the buildings in Rowan County, partly because he was a Republican dealing with a Democratic administration in Washington, DC, and in Frankfort.) The buildings were moved out of Rowan County to the Lincoln Institute of Kentucky at Lincoln Ridge in

Roy Cornette, Superintendent of Schools during Depression years. Salary reduced from $175.00 to $100.00 per month.

Shelby County. They were used to house African Americans training in a radio school for the Lexington Signal Depot.

The New Deal programs prompted Rowan County leaders to think boldly and clearly. Also, credit or blame, depending on your point of view, must be given to those political and educational leaders who tried to live up to President Roosevelt's original idea that, "all projects should be highly constructive, permanent, and add to the wealth of the state."

During the Great Depression, Americans learned to sacrifice and live without many of the basic necessities of life. Young men left home and hearth to join the Civilian Conservation Corps (CCC). Over half of their $21.00 per month was sent home to their families. Many fathers were separated from their families and lived temporarily in other communities where they might be able to find work in order to hack out an existence and send a few dollars home.

All of these difficulties of family life would be intensified during the WWII when food, clothing, gas, rubber, and other materials were rationed. And when there would be tremendous housing shortages. Young men would leave home and enter the military service to defend their country. Others would leave home to work in defense plants. During WWII, for the first time, women would leave home to work in defense plants and, later on, many would enter military service. They were not sent into combat, but women in the military

Busy activity along Haldeman, Kentucky, Main Street, 1930s. *Photo: Becker Family.*

service in WWII were intended to release men into combat. The sacrifices made by Americans during the Great Depression turned out to be a period of "basic training." These privations helped to prepare Americans for the suffering, sacrifice and separation that WWII would bring.

Haldeman's Community Christmas Tree, highlight of holiday season during Depression.

## CHAPTER 2

# CCC Camps: Preparation for War

"When ye hear of wars and rumors of war be not dismayed" (Luke 13:7)

Of the many alphabet agencies that helped bring us through the Great Depression, the CCC was the first to arrive in Rowan County. It taught us something about discipline in our daily lives. The Civilian Conservation Corps (CCC) was a quasi-military organization for young men. They operated on military time (24-hour clock); they lived in military style barracks under a full military style discipline. Most bases were commanded by former military officers. The CCC workers, even though they didn't know it, they were being prepared for military service. While at the same time making a valuable contribution to improve the economy. They also were helping to preserve our national infrastructure.

The hills and hollows of Rowan County, Kentucky, known for their scenic beauty and the timber they produce, were somewhat isolated from their neighbors. But in the early 1900s most of the old growth timber had been marketed, and the forests had not been restored. However, by the 1930s, conservation began to enter our vocabulary, and thoughts began turning to ways of preserving forest land from fire and erosion.

After President Franklin D. Roosevelt was elected by a landslide on November 8, 1932 (he carried all but six states), his first priority was to get this nation's economy moving. Declaring, "All we have to fear is fear itself," he began formulating legislation designed to put poor people to work, instead of giving them monthly "relief checks." Although it was a government payroll, they were working and not drawing what was called "rocking chair" money.

## CCC AUTHORIZED BY CONGRESS

With conservation a key plank in his platform, President Roosevelt succeeded in getting Congress to pass his Emergency Conservation Act. On March 31, 1933, Congress authorized the President to employ unemployed citizens to help restore the nation's depleted natural resources, and to establish an orderly work program of useful public work. Thus, the Civilian Conservation Corps was born.

The CCC was a timely organization, designed to give boys and young men the dignity of work, by building bridges, roads, trails, fire towers, and at the same time, conserving the forests. It also helped to reduce relief rolls, and provided a basic introduction into a disciplined military life. To join, you had to be at least 17 years old. You could enlist for six months, with an option of re-enlisting for another six months. They lived on base in a military barracks, and ate in the mess hall. They were not permitted off their base without a pass. Their housing, food, and clothes were all furnished and they each were paid $30 a month, of which $25 was sent home to their family. (Later on the youngsters got to keep $8 dollars, and sent home $22.) Most said they felt rich every payday.

## CCC CAMP ARRIVES IN ROWAN

On December 4, 1933, the federal CCC legislation reached Rowan

CCC Camp F-4 established at Morgan Fork, Rowan County, Kentucky, December 1933.

County when Camp F 4, Company 578 was established at Clearfield, Kentucky. It was located on what is now State Road 519, at the foot of Clack Mountain. However, the government began purchasing private land in 1930, and the Cumberland National Forest (now Daniel Boone) was growing. Also, the CCC Camp soon began to outgrow the base on Morgan Fork.

Mrs. Chadima, a widow with several children, had a small farm east of Morehead up Rodburn Hollow. In 1935, the federal government decided that was where the new CCC Camp would be built. After Mrs. Chadima turned down the government offer for her farm, she was sued, and the land was taken from her, under the law of eminent domain. I had just joined the cub scouts and the scoutmaster was her son, Joe Chadima. When he told us he was leaving Morehead because the Government had taken his home, we could not understand a government like that—and were

CCC Camp F-4 moved to Rodburn Hollow in 1935.

heart-broken because he was leaving. He later joined the CCCs, figuring if he could not "lick 'em, he'd join 'em."

On November 19, 1936, CCC Camp F 4, Company 578, was moved from Morgan Fork to Rodburn Hollow. The number of workers in the camp eventually grew to 470. That camp was responsible for maintaining the National Forest land in Rowan, Menifee, Morgan, Elliott, and portions of Fleming and Bath Counties. That amounted to a total of 281,507 acres of forest land.

### FOREST FIRES FIRST PRIORITY

The first priority of the CCC was fighting forest fires, in an area that was once a great hardwood lumber center. When the government purchased the logged-out land from private landowners the goal was to protect the forests so that new stands of hardwood would grow, and a system of perpetual timber harvesting established. Forest fires were rampant in Rowan County in those days. Keeping the fire from destroying the timber was difficult and doubtful. But the CCC was making progress. In 1933 there were 3,000 acres burned in that region, compared to 610 acres in 1937. Fires were mostly man-made,

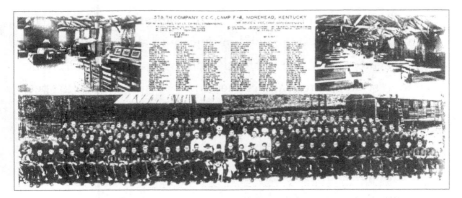

Camp F-4 personnel grew to 450 in 1936.

either accidentally or on purpose. Sadly, some locals would set forest fires just to see the CCC boys and men work to fight them. A few were prosecuted, but not nearly all who should've been.

### BUILD FIRE TOWERS AND PHONE LINES

The steel fire towers constructed at McCauley Ridge, Hickory Flats, Tater Knob and Triangle were a key element in forest fire protection. The towers were 40 feet tall and 14 feet by 14 feet square. Each tower contained two cots, a stove, table and stool. The one closest to Morehead was the Triangle tower, on top of the mountain just off Dry Creek Road. Some of the towers, such as the Tater Knob tower, were built in such isolated areas that the only way you could get materials there was by mule. Tater Knob the most famous one locally, was located just across the Licking River near Yale, Kentucky in Bath County. Harvard Alfrey was a long time firewatcher and at one time he and his wife lived in the tower. The Tater Knob tower has now been restored, and is worth the trip to visit. There you can see how it contributed to the safety of the forest.

When it was first built, CCC boys strung telephone lines to the tower. The lines connected the tower to the camp, so that the fire alarm and site could be phoned in quickly to allow the CCC boys to get a head start on fire fighting. There were a total of 12 phones located in strategic areas and connected by 40 miles of line to speed up reporting the fires. A very important firefighting tool was the "alidade" or fire finder located in each tower. It used triangulation to pinpoint fires. When you stop to realize there were no phones in these rural areas in 1937, this was a monumental move forward in communications and firefighting.

## HIKING TO TRIANGLE TOWER

Years after it was built, the Triangle tower held a certain mysterious, yet romantic attraction for the young people growing up in Morehead during that era. It was an annual rite of spring for classes to hike up to that tower. To get there, you crossed Triplett Creek at the dam, and walked up the hollow, climbed the mountain and then followed the ridge until you reached the tower. Then you climbed the rickety steps to the top of the swaying tower. Then you would walk around the outside platform, feeling like you were master of all you surveyed. The view was breathtaking. Almost every class at Breckinridge and Morehead Consolidated made the journey at least once. Hiking to Triangle Tower was considered one rite of passage to every child in Morehead. You had to or you were called "chicken" or even worse. On the trip you passed a huge rock overhang in which tobacco was sometimes hung for curing. One Breck student fell out of that natural tobacco barn and broke his leg and had to be carried back.

## LOCAL BOYS JOIN CCC

Enrollment in the Morehead CCC Camp reached its peak of 470

Triangle Fire Tower built by CCC boys near Morehead, Kentucky.

men in 1938. Many men from Rowan County joined for at least one six-month hitch. Some were stationed in Rowan County. Others joined and were sent to far off places. My uncle, Norton Earley, joined on his seventeenth birthday and was sent to Montana, where he spent a year clearing forests of dead trees, fighting forest fires, and building roads and bridges. Phil Hardin, another Rowan resident, joined thinking he would see the world (he lied about his age so he could join at age 16). Instead, he was sent to Pike County and served his time there. Some fatherless children could join at age 16 under a special hardship ruling. Ralph Earley joined and spent two years in the CCC and still was not old enough to enter military service. But practically every one of these CCC boys soon was in the military after being discharged from the CCC camp.

While researching this chapter of Rowan County's history, I came across a copy of my father's discharge from the CCC Camp in Morehead. Lon Ellis—serial number CC5-162897—was honorably discharged September 30, 1937, at the expiration of his enlistment. I was 10 years old when my father was in the CCCs. Some married men with special skills were accepted and allowed to live off base. They received their clothing and were issued a weekly food supply to take home. We were very poor in those days and that food my dad brought home went a long way. I can still remember the taste of those canned pears in syrup, and the fresh oranges and bananas.

**IDENTIFYING AND NAMING PHYSICAL LANDMARKS**

At one time one of my father's jobs was riding horseback over the county to identify and mark on a map the names of creeks, roads and hills. It was only then I found out where Wilson Hill was on Licking River although I was living right beside it. Dad was paid $30 a month plus $8 expenses for his horse.

II 5

# Certificate of Discharge
## from
## Civilian Conservation Corps

TO ALL WHOM IT MAY CONCERN:

THIS IS TO CERTIFY THAT * ___Lon Ellis, CC5-162897L___ , A MEMBER OF THE

CIVILIAN CONSERVATION CORPS, WHO WAS ENROLLED ___October 8, 1935___ AT
<small>(Date)</small>

___CCC Co 578, Clearfield, Kentucky___ , IS HEREBY HONORABLY DISCHARGED THEREFROM, BY REASON

OF ** ___EXPIRATION OF TERM OF ENROLLMENT___

SAID ___Lon Ellis___ WAS BORN IN ___Cogswell___ ,

IN THE STATE OF ___Kentucky___ WHEN ENROLLED HE WAS ___Thirty-one___ YEARS

OF AGE AND BY OCCUPATION A ___Tractor Man___ HE HAD ___Blue___ EYES,

___Brown___ HAIR, ___Ruddy___ COMPLEXION, AND WAS ___Five___ FEET

___Four and one-half___ INCHES IN HEIGHT. HIS COLOR WAS ___White___

GIVEN UNDER MY HAND AT ___Morehead, Kentucky___ , THIS ___30th___ DAY

OF ___September___ , ONE THOUSAND NINE HUNDRED AND ___Thirty-Seven___

C.C.C. Form No. 2
April 5, 1933

\* Insert name, as "John J. Doe".
\*\* Give reason for discharge.

3—10171

___(Name)___ ___(Title)___
ROY M. WILLIAMS
FIRST LIEUT. COAST ARTILLERY—RESERVE
COMMANDING

Lon Ellis's certificate of discharge from CC Corps.

II 6

## RECORD OF SERVICE IN CIVILIAN CONSERVATION CORPS

** Served:

a. From 10/8/35 to 3/31/36, under War Dept. at Clearfield, Ky.

Type of work Labor *Manner of performance Satisfactory

b. From 4/1/36 to 9/30/36, under War Dept. at Clearfield, Ky.

Type of work Labor *Manner of performance Satisfactory

c. From 10/1/36 to 11/20/36, under War Dept. at Clearfield, Ky.

Type of work Labor *Manner of performance Satisfactory

d. From 11/21/36 to 3/31/37, under War Dept. at Morehead, Ky.

Type of work Fire Patrolman *Manner of performance Satisfactory

e. From 4/1/37 to 9/30/37, under War Dept. at Morehead, Ky.

Type of work Fire Patrolman *Manner of performance Satisfactory

Remarks: Provisions of Federal Compensation Act has been read to this man.

Enrollee notified of ineligibility for reselection for a period of six
months from date of discharge.
AWOL: None.
AWOP: None.
ELWP: 7/6-12/35

IMMUNIZATION COMPLETED DATE 10/21/35
TYPHOID & PARA-TYPHOID 10/21/35
SMALLPOX 10/8/35

SELECTING AGENCY NOTIFIED
OF DISCHARGE DATE 9/30/37

HAS BEEN ADVISED OF REGULATIONS CONCERNING
NON-ELEGIBILITY FOR RE-ENROLLMENT

Qualifications: Laborer

Discharged: September 30, 1937 at Morehead, Kentucky

Transportation furnished from None furnished. Local Experienced Enrollee

(Name) ROY M. WILLIAMS (Title)
FIRST LIEUT. COAST ARTILLERY—RESERVE
COMMANDING

*Use words "Excellent", "Satisfactory", or "Unsatisfactory"
*To be taken from C.C.C. Form No. 1.

FORT THOMAS, KY.
OCT 8 1937

Lon Ellis's service record in CC Corps 1935 - 1937.

Among other land marks on the map were Scotts Creek, Ramey's Creek, and Clay Lick, along with hundreds of others that were identified. Also, at one time, a part of his job was being a firewatcher. It was then he spent some time in Tater Knob tower. It was a lonely life on top of that mountain for several days at a time. Occasionally I would go to the fire tower and spend the night with him.

When the CCC men were building the bridge over Licking River into Menifee County, my father was assigned as a night watchman on weekends to protect all the material and equipment on the construction site. He allowed me to come and spend a few nights with him there, and we did some night fishing.

## CCC BOYS NOT ALWAYS ACCEPTED

Dr. Kenneth Jones, was a retired chiropractor, joined the CCC Camp at Rodburn when he was age 17. He also hoped to see the wild west, but was sent to the mountains of Southern Kentucky at Camp Bledsoe. He said the CCC boys were courting all the local girls, thereby making the local boys very unhappy. On one occasion while the CCC boys were working on a road, those mad mountaineers starting shooting at them from the brush. (I'm sure those mountaineers didn't mean to kill any of the CCC crew because they were all marksmen and could've easily injured any of the workers if that was really their goal.) The men jumped in their truck and returned to camp and got their pistols from their barracks bag, returning to work, and returning fire when fired upon. That camp was quickly closed, and the boys transferred to Junction City, Kentucky.

While the CCC camp was in Clearfield, Kentucky, there were lots of bad feelings between the local boys and the CCC boys. The Clearfield boys let it be known that the CCC boys were not allowed to cross Dry Creek. While the camp was in Clearfield the rule was strictly enforced by the local boys. Which may have been one reason the camp was moved to Rodburn Hollow.

The Morehead Camp established a side camp at the mouth of Murder Branch in Menifee County. About 75 men were stationed there for three years before closing it and transferring the men back to Morehead. There were no murders there; the creek was named after an Indian massacre of white settlers on that spot in the late 1700s.

## CCC CONTRIBUTED TO FUTURE OF ROWAN

Most of the young men who joined the CCCs were unemployed, or eking out an existence by farming. Rowan County had a 51% unemployment rate. The economic outlook was bleak and jobs were few. You could get a discharge from the CCC if you found employment or returned to school. But most families in Rowan County were too proud to go "on relief." That was a government handout, and they wanted no part of it. Although the Rowan County Brick and Tile Plants were open they were operating at 50% capacity. Most CCC boys were hard working, poor people deserving of assistance. The CCC permitted pride of purpose, keeping families from starving, giving gainful employment to the unemployed, and contributing beyond anyone's imagination to the future of Rowan County.

## MANY ROADS AND BRIDGES BUILT BY CCC

By 1938, the CCCs had strung 40 miles of telephone lines, built 45 miles of year round (limestone gravel) roads. They had constructed fire towers, and bridges. They built all-weather gravel roads to some of the most isolated and inaccessible areas of Rowan County. They built a road over Clack Mountain, and out Pretty Ridge, down Clay

Bridge across Licking River built by CC Corps. (Men later built bridges during WWII.)

Lick to the Menifee County line. Also, they built the Lockege Road, which ran down to the old Cogswell Post Office, and Alfrey School. And they constructed the CCC Trail from Clearfield to Elliottville, plus many other roads.

As a 10-year-old boy, I lived on Clay Lick Creek. Because of the depression, my father lost his job at the local Red Rose Dairy and joined the CCCs. My mother was not employed as a teacher that year, so we had to move back to the farm. I remember the talk of an all weather road being built in front of our house, and that summer I could hear the blasting and dozing as it slowly inched toward out house. One day the bulldozer got closer and closer. Excitedly I sat out in the front yard waiting breathlessly for the first signs that progress was coming our way. Suddenly the first dozer came crashing out of the trees on the side of the hill pushing a load of dirt in front of it. The dozer was driven by Gilbert Jones, and we were now on a gravel road to Morehead. That road made it possible for me to continue school at Breckinridge by riding in cattle trucks to school. My mother would awaken me at 5:30 a.m., and after a hearty country breakfast, I would walk out to the road and wait for the cattle truck that was my means of transportation for the 14 miles into Morehead on a curvy gravel road. The truck had an open wooden slat bed, topped with a tarpaulin folded down the sides and tied tightly. I would climb into the truck and sit with my back against the cab. There were usually six or eight men in the truck that worked at the Clearfield tile plant or attended college. The driver had two daughters that rode in the cab to go to Morehead High School. After school, I would walk down to Morehead High School and wait with the truck driver's daughters for our ride home. This system worked fairly well, even though I was usually covered with a lot of limestone dust.

As the weather got colder, even though I was dressed warmly and covered with blankets in the back of the truck, it became a cold ride. I was glad when Christmas vacation came. However, during that time I was extremely ill. I missed Christmas completely that year because I was in and out of consciousness. My parents said I was out of my head. But a couple of days after Christmas, old Dr. Homer Nickell made a house call and examined me. His diagnosis was intestinal flu, and he gave me some pills that must have helped me survive even though I did miss the first of what would be many Christmases I was destined to miss throughout my lifetime. When Christmas vacation ended, I was still recuperating from my bout with the flu. Therefore, my mother, concerned for my health, and the fact I had to ride in the back of a cattle truck the rest of the winter, kept me out of school for the remainder of the school year. During that time I attended her class in the one-room rural school where she was teaching. I don't know which was worse, walking over a mile to the top of a hill to the one-room school that winter, or riding in the back of a cattle truck the 14 miles to Morehead each day. But I survived and she tutored me the rest of the year.

By the time the next school year began, we had moved back into Morehead. When I returned to school that fall, I expected to repeat a grade. However, I was not happy with my new classmates. My sensitive teacher must have realized this, and after I was in that class for about two weeks, I was moved up to the next grade with my former classmates. That was a happy day in my life!

## CCC HELPED EDUCATION AND ECONOMY

It is impossible to measure the economic, educational, social, and cultural impact the CCCs had upon this county and region. The high correlation between the roads constructed by the CCC Camp and the increased enrollment at Morehead State College should be noted. CCC roads were built in all the surrounding counties. Before these roads were built, there were many people in Rowan County and nearby counties who wanted to attend college but could not. They could not afford to board in town, and the roads were impassable in winter. The road from Morehead to Frenchburg, and the bridge across Licking River reduced the distance from Morehead to Frenchburg from 84 miles to 34 miles. Rural mail delivery was established as a result of these roads being built. Homes and schools began to appear along those gravel roads. Of course, the limestone dust was terrible during dry weather. Although people choked breathing the dust, they did not complain. Some poured oil in front of their homes to reduce dust. Morehead became much more of a business center, as well as an educational center with the establishment of these connecting, year round, gravel roads.

Education important—recruits taught by local teachers.

## PREPARED BOYS FOR MILITARY SERVICE

The CCC program was administered by the War Department in Washington, DC, and the men in charge were all either officers in the R.O.T.C., regular Army or retired Army Engineers, recalled for this special duty. The engineers provided the skills needed for the construction of roads and bridges. In Rowan County, local physician Dr. E.D. Blair was appointed military surgeon, and he was the one who helped keep the men healthy. The surgeon reported that each man averaged gaining eight pounds while in the CCCs. Because the discipline, drilling, working, eating, and sleeping were all according to military discipline, these young men were getting in shape for military service in WWII, only a few years in the future. Those who had experienced CCC Camp service adapted much quicker to military life when they were called into WWII.

CIVILIAN CONSERVATION CORPS
COMPANY 578, CAMP F-4
Office of the Camp Commander
CLEARFIELD, KENTUCKY

October 31, 1934

SUBJECT:  Hallowe'en Party.

TO    :

    1.  Pursuant to authority contained in War Department Regulat-
ions, CCC, dated September 1, 1934, report that there will be given,
by the members of this organization, one (1) Hallowe'en Party, on the
evening of this date to which you are cordially invited to attend.

    2.  It being impractical for all guests to furnish their own
transportation, the Quartermaster of this camp will, upon your reques
furnish necessary transportation, without delay, to this station, and
return.

    3.  Request acknowledgment of invitation by presentation of this
communication at the door.

          By order of Captain ARTHUR S. ROTHROCK:

JOHN L ADAMS
1st Lt. FA-Res
Adjutant

OFFICIAL:
    JOHN L ADAMS
    1st Lt. FA-Res
      Adjutant
DISTRIBUTION:
1 - Acting Quartermaster
1 - Welfare Officer
1 - Mess Officer
1 - Educational Adviser
1 - Each Guest
1 - File

Social events important part of CCC Program.

## EDUCATION AVAILABLE

    The CCC hired unemployed teachers to teach the young men
in the camps. They conducted classes in literature, reading, writing,

Tater Knob Fire Tower as it appeared in the 1930's.

leadership, journalism, forestry, typing, first aid, photography, personal development, cooking, baking and many other areas of learning. Each inductee was required to attend three hours per week in classes. The local educational advisor was Earl C. May. Local teachers included Sam Johnson, Catherine Caudill, Mary Olive Boggess, Anna Lee Barry, Minnie Gastineau and Bernice Barker. A cooking class was offered on the campus of Morehead State College, and 28 men from surrounding camps attended because good cooking was very important to camp morale.

In addition to education, recreation was an important part of camp life. Pool and ping-pong tables, horseshoe pits, monopoly and many other games were provided as a part of the recreation center on base. Also, local ministers provided church services. *The Happy Days* magazine, the official publication of the national CCC Camps, included an article in the February 10, 1938, issue proclaiming the excellent educational opportunities at the Morehead Camp. The publication also commended the officers: Lt. Roy S. Williams, Commanding Officer, Dr. Everett Blair, Camp Surgeon, Bruce L. Vice Superintendent, and Earl May, Educational Advisor. It seemed that Morehead's camp was one of the nation's best.

## ATTEMPT TO CLOSE CAMP REJECTED

In 1938, an effort to close the Camp at Morehead brought an outcry from Morehead to Washington and back. A local committee was formed to combat the Camp closing. That committee included Senator Alben W. Barkley (later Vice President), Congressman Fred M. Vinson (later Chief Justice of the U.S. Supreme Court), and lo-

Breath-taking view from top of Tater Knob Tower.

cal men: H.C. Haggan, Jack Wilson and W.E. Crutcher. Through their efforts the camp remained open until the beginning of WWII in 1941.

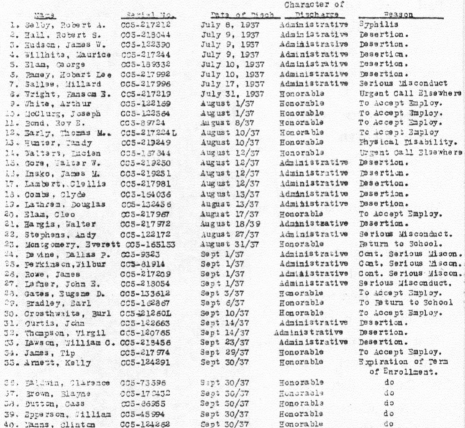

Civilian Conservation Corps
Headquarters
Company 578 CCC Camp F-4
Morehead, Kentucky

ENROLLEE LOSSES

July 1 - - - September 30/37

| Name | Serial No. | Date of Disch | Character of Discharge | Reason |
|---|---|---|---|---|
| 1. Selby, Robert A. | CC5-217212 | July 8, 1937 | Administrative | Syphilis |
| 2. Hall, Robert S. | CC5-213044 | July 9, 1937 | Administrative | Desertion. |
| 3. Hudson, James W. | CC5-122390 | July 9, 1937 | Administrative | Desertion. |
| 4. Willhite, Maurice | CC5-217244 | July 9, 1937 | Administrative | Desertion. |
| 5. Elam, George | CC5-189332 | July 10, 1937 | Administrative | Desertion. |
| 6. Ramey, Hobart Lee | CC5-217992 | July 10, 1937 | Administrative | Desertion. |
| 7. Salee, Millard | CC5-217996 | July 17, 1937 | Administrative | Serious Misconduct |
| 8. Wright, Ransom B. | CC5-217219 | July 31, 1937 | Honorable | Urgent Call Elsewhere |
| 9. White, Arthur | CC5-122169 | August 1/37 | Honorable | To Accept Employ. |
| 10. McClurg, Joseph | CC5-122564 | August 1/37 | Honorable | To Accept Employ. |
| 11. Bond, Roy E. | CC5-89724 | August 8/37 | Honorable | To Accept Employ. |
| 12. Early, Thomas M. | CC5-217224 L | August 10/37 | Honorable | To Accept Employ |
| 13. Hunter, Tandy | CC5-213249 | August 10/37 | Honorable | Physical Disability. |
| 14. Walters, Lucien | CC5-157344 | August 12/37 | Honorable | Urgent Call Elsewhere |
| 15. Gore, Walter W. | CC5-213250 | August 12/37 | Administrative | Desertion. |
| 16. Insko, James M. | CC5-219251 | August 12/37 | Administrative | Desertion. |
| 17. Lambert, Clellis | CC5-217981 | August 12/37 | Administrative | Desertion. |
| 18. Combs, Clyde | CC5-164036 | August 13/37 | Administrative | Desertion. |
| 19. Lathrem, Douglas | CC5-132456 | August 13/37 | Administrative | Desertion. |
| 20. Elam, Cleo | CC5-217967 | August 17/37 | Honorable | To Accept Employ. |
| 21. Hargis, Walter | CC5-217972 | August 18/39 | Administrative | Desertion. |
| 22. Stephens, Andy | CC5-122172 | August 27/37 | Administrative | Serious Misconduct. |
| 23. Montgomery, Everett | CC5-165153 | August 31/37 | Honorable | Return to School. |
| 24. Devine, Dallas P. | CC5-9323 | Sept 1/37 | Administrative | Cont. Serious Miscon. |
| 25. Perkinson, Wilbur | CC5-81914 | Sept 1/37 | Administrative | Cont. Serious Miscon. |
| 26. Rowe, James | CC5-217209 | Sept 1/37 | Administrative | Cont. Serious Miscon. |
| 27. Lefner, John B. | CC5-213054 | Sept 1/37 | Administrative | Serious Misconduct. |
| 28. Gates, Eugene D. | CC5-133612 | Sept 3/37 | Honorable | To Accept Employ. |
| 29. Bradley, Earl | CC5-162867 | Sept 6/37 | Honorable | To Return to School |
| 30. Crosthwaite, Burl | CC5-21260L | Sept 10/37 | Honorable | To Accept Employ. |
| 31. Curtis, John | CC5-122663 | Sept 14/37 | Administrative | Desertion. |
| 32. Thompson, Virgil | CC5-120765 | Sept 14/37 | Administrative | Desertion. |
| 33. Lawson, William C. | CC5-213456 | Sept 23/37 | Administrative | Desertion. |
| 34. James, Tip | CC5-217974 | Sept 29/37 | Honorable | To Accept Employ. |
| 35. Arnett, Kelly | CC5-124291 | Sept 30/37 | Honorable | Expiration of Term of Enrollment. |
| 36. Baldwin, Clarence | CC5-73596 | Sept 30/37 | Honorable | do |
| 37. Brown, Blayne | CC5-170432 | Sept 30/37 | Honorable | do |
| 38. Dutton, Cass | CC5-86355 | Sept 30/37 | Honorable | do |
| 39. Epperson, William | CC5-45994 | Sept 30/37 | Honorable | do |
| 40. Manns, Clinton | CC5-124262 | Sept 30/37 | Honorable | do |

- 1 -

| Name | Serial No. | Date of Disch | Character of Discharge | Reason |
|---|---|---|---|---|
| 41. Phillips, Emory C. | CC5-162478 | Sept 30/37 | Honorable | Expiration of Term of Enrollment |
| 42. Stamper, Fay | CC5-124326 | Sept 30/37 | Honorable | do |
| 43. Tankersley, William | CC5-103095 | Sept 30/37 | Honorable | do |
| 44. Conn, Wilbert | CC5-216085 | Sept 30/37 | Honorable | do |
| 45. Cox, Elmer | CC5-101327 | Sept 30/37 | Honorable | do |
| 46. Fannin, Green | CC5-24221 | Sept 30/37 | Honorable | do |
| 47. Karrick, James H. | CC5-217980 | Sept 30/37 | Honorable | do |
| 48. Mays, Sylvester | CC5-24222 | Sept 30/37 | Honorable | do |
| 49. Mocabee, James E. | CC5-217985 | Sept 30/37 | Honorable | do |
| 50. Perry, William | CC5-217988 | Sept 30/37 | Honorable | do |
| 51. Phelps, Daniel M. | CC5-217990 | Sept 30/37 | Honorable | do |
| 52. Puckett, Bert | CC5-122556 | Sept 30/37 | Honorable | do |
| 53. Shrout, Earl W. | CC5-217214 | Sept 30/37 | Honorable | do |
| 54. White, Clifton | CC5-120803 | Sept 30/37 | Honorable | do |
| 55. White, Darrell | CC5-218969 | Sept 30/37 | Honorable | do |
| 56. White, John L. | CC5-162875 | Sept 30/37 | Honorable | do |
| 57. Ellis, Lon | CC5-162897L | Sept 30/37 | Honorable | do |
| 58. Fraley, Fay | CC5-164806L | Sept 30/37 | Honorable | do |
| 59. Haney, Perry | CC5-162877L | Sept 30/37 | Honorable | do |
| 60. Roberts, Cleo | CC5-217558L | Sept 30/37 | Honorable | do |
| 61. Roberts, Orville | CC5-107904L | Sept 30/37 | Honorable | do |
| 62. Rogers, David C. | CC5-121264L | Sept 30/37 | Honorable | do |
| 63. Thomas, David | CC5-217220L | Sept 30/37 | Honorable | do |

Report made by. T. J. McCoy

The Civilian Conservation Corps was of inestimable value to Rowan County. Forest fires became almost a thing of the past, and the hills began to grow timber again. Proper harvesting of timber was initiated. New roads and bridges gave outlets to people who had previously been trapped all winter in the most isolated areas. The CCC Camp in Rowan County had a major impact upon the economic, educational, cultural, social, and recreational growth of this area. The site of the old CCC Camp at Rodburn Hollow now belongs to the city of Morehead, Kentucky. It was obtained through a land exchange with the U.S. Government, and is now a part of the City of Morehead Parks and Recreation Department. It includes a well-maintained camp ground and lovely picnic area, in recognition of the historical importance of this site to the people of the county.

# 578th COMPANY
# CCC CAMP F 4
**Morehead, Kentucky**
**1933 - 1940**
**Established December 4, 1933**

*Some of the Rowan Countians*
*Who Were Members of the CCC: Camp F4*

| | |
|---|---|
| Harvard Alfrey | Perry Haney |
| Charles Fraley | Tip James |
| Earl Bradley | Robert Linville |
| Virgil Caudill | John Litton |
| Murvel E. Caudill | Merle Martin |
| Joe Chadima | John J. Mauk |
| Virgil Conn | Bert Puckett |
| William Crum | Joe Rice |
| Burl Crosthwaite | Ollie Roberts |
| Thomas Early | Ray Stamper |
| Lon Ellis | John Swim |
| Elmer Gulley | Clyde Tackett |

Virgil Thompson

**CHAPTER 3**

# A Pearl Harbor Christmas, 1941

"When you shall hear of wars and commotions be not terrified:
for these things must first come to pass." (Luke 21:9)

Christmas is a meaningful time of rich remembering, and almost everyone has vivid memories of a special Christmas past. With apologies to Ebenezer Scrooge and Charles Dickens, I would like to recall some ghosts of Christmas past, of a time like our country had never known before, and may never know again.

The year was 1941, and the ghost of war was very real in my hometown of Morehead, Rowan County, in Appalachian Kentucky. That was America's first Christmas to be locked in combat in the global conflict of World War II.

## LIVES LOST BEFORE DECEMBER 7, 1941

In early December, even before the war began, the U.S. Navy had lost its first warship in the battle of the Atlantic. The USS Reuben James was sunk by a German submarine off the coast of Iceland with 76 men lost out of a crew of 110.

Although tensions were mounting between the U.S. and Japan, diplomatic talks were continuing. Even as Japanese troops were

**Honolulu Star-Bulletin 1st EXTRA**

**WAR!**

Associated Press by Transpacific Telephone

SAN FRANCISCO, Dec. 7.—President Roosevelt announced this morning that Japanese planes had attacked Manila and Pearl Harbor

**OAHU BOMBED BY JAPANESE PLANES**

KNOWN DEAD, INJURED, AT EMERGENCY HOSPITAL

**Attack Made On Island's Defense Areas**

**Hundreds See City Bombed**

slaughtering the Chinese, U.S. Secretary of State Cordell Hull urged the Japanese to end their hostilities with China. Relations with Germany were also almost at the breaking point.

At daybreak on Sunday, December 7, 1941, "a date that will live in infamy," 360 Japanese war planes secretly took off from six aircraft carriers 300 miles from Hawaii. They succeeded in reaching the U.S. Naval Base at Pearl Harbor undetected and pulverized the Naval and Army bases on the island. After two hours of unrelenting bombing and strafing, the sneak attack decimated the military bases on the island. The Japanese attack sunk or seriously damaged eight U.S. battleships and 14 smaller ships. Their continuous dive-bombing and strafing left 2,400 Americans dead and 1,300 wounded. The

Airbase at Pearl Harbor almost destroyed December 7, 1941.

attack succeeded in almost destroying many of the military bases on the island. At the sudden tragedy of burning battleships, painfully wounded soldiers, sailors, civilians and unrecognizable corpses, America was stunned.

It was the full intention of fanatic Japanese warlords to destroy America's resolve and ability to wage war with that one sneak attack. Even though they succeeded in sinking or seriously damaging much

John D. Barker survived Pearl Harbor attack.

of the U.S. Pacific Fleet; even though they killed or wounded 3,700 soldiers, sailors and civilians; and, even though many bodies were unrecognizable and never recovered, that attack was unsuccessful because it did not deter America's ability to make war.

Admiral Yamamato, who led the Japanese attack said, "I fear all we have done is awaken a sleeping giant." How prophetic that statement turned out to be. That "sleeping giant" called America rose from the rubble of Pearl Harbor to defend to the death our way of life. "Remember Pearl Harbor" became the battle cry of the troops throughout the war, reminding Americans that freedom is never free, its cost sometimes measured in blood, sacrifice and tears.

A few days later, Germany and Italy joined Japan as the Axis nations declared war upon the United States, resulting in a global conflict between the Allies—the U.S., Britain, France, Russia, and 27 other nations. The Axis powers included Germany, Italy and Japan and eight other nations. It all started on "Sad Sunday," December 7, 1941, and exploded into a worldwide conflict. Many Americans living at that time never forgot where they were and what they were doing when the news reached them that this nation's innocence,

Scene on lawn of private home, Honolulu, December 7, 1941.

complacency and security had been breached, and how that sad Sunday in 1941 affected their lives.

## MEMORIES OF PEARL HARBOR DAY

The first Sunday of December, 1941, I was a fourteen-year-old sophomore at Breckinridge High School in Morehead, deep in the heartland of America, far from the ravages of war. The small college town of Morehead had a population of about 2,000 people. Breckinridge was the college's 12-grade demonstration school. I had attended the school for 10 years. There were about 300 students in the school, and we were like family because most of us had been together since the first grade.

Each December Breckinridge High School presented an annual minstrel program. It was the highlight of the school year and was always an eagerly anticipated event. We were practicing the

Bomb fragments killed three innocent civilians in sedan, December 7, 1941.

program that fateful Sunday afternoon when two older boys, J.B Calvert, Jr. and George McCullough came into the building and announced that Pearl Harbor had been bombed by the Japanese with great loss of life. George McCullough would later be killed in the Pacific, and J.B. would serve three years in the war. In fact, every boy in that minstrel production would end up serving in the military during WWII.

On that sad Sunday everyone went home immediately after hearing the news and stayed glued to the radio for any information we could get. What we gleaned from the static filled airwaves from radio station WLW in Cincinnati, Ohio, was sketchy and confusing because of military censorship. It was not until weeks later when we could see newsreels of the devastation resulting from the attack that the full impact of the sneak attack was known to the American people.

In December, 1941, still grieving, this nation was united as it never had been before. A song entitled "Remember Pearl Harbor" was popular. The first two lines said, "Remember Pearl Harbor as we go to meet the foes; let's remember Pearl Harbor as we did the Alamo." That song was on the lips of many American soldiers, throughout WWII, especially when the going was tough. The Japanese attack on Pearl Harbor that brought the United States into WWIIresulted in the sacrifice of 400 thousand young American lives before the conflict ended.

Lt. George McCullough, Jr. only child of Morehead's Fire Chief KIA WWII, Pacific.

## PEACE TIME PURSUITS TO WAR WORRIES

Christmas was approaching and our little town was pursuing a path of peace on earth and good will toward all men. Although war was raging around the world, we were at peace in our land and churches were practicing their Christmas programs. Schools were preparing their Christmas plays, and everyone was planning a joyous Christmas season as our nation recovered from the depression. Although we did not realize it, our lives were about to change forever.

Left to right, top to bottom: Ligon Kessler, Claude Kessler, Robert Lee "Pete" Kessler—these brothers from Morehead joined different branches of the military soon after Pearl Harbor. All three survived the war.

Those who attended church on Sunday morning on December 7, 1941, were smiling happily, never dreaming that in a few hours their smiles would be wiped away perhaps for years to come. It was about 2:00 p.m. local time when the ominous news came. On that day, millions of light-hearted American boys and girls who had never known real responsibility changed instantly into serious-minded Americans who all asked the same question, "What can I do?" We did not know what the war was all about and many of us did not believe in war. But we were ready to fight and die if necessary so that this nation could remain free. We somehow realized we would never again be the same innocent carefree, yes, naive individuals we were prior to Sunday, December 7, 1941.

(Top) Walter W. Carr and (bottom) Robert B. Hogge joined the military soon after Pearl Harbor.

On Monday, President Franklin D. Roosevelt, in a joint session of Congress, declared war on Japan. On Tuesday, Germany and Italy declared war on the United States broadening the conflict.

The whole nation was in a somber mood in 1941. U.S. troops were being overrun by the Japanese at Bataan, Wake Island and Guam. Then, on December 25,

# New Pastor To Open With Revival Meet

Reverend Ramah Johnson's first Sunday as pastor of the Morehead First Church of God, December 7, 1941.

the British colony of Hong Kong fell to 38 divisions of Japanese troops.

Germany and Italy had declared all out war on the U.S. and our allies. However, President Roosevelt in one of his memorable fireside chats assured this nation that, "With the help of Almighty God, we shall ultimately prevail."

## NATIONAL PRAYER FOR OUR PRESIDENT

When we returned to school on December 8, the students at my high school were permitted to go into our Social Studies classroom and listen to the latest news on the school radio which we had purchased with the profits we made from selling candy at school. That day we heard President Roosevelt address a joint session of Congress with his historic declaration of war. He opened his speech with these historic words: "Yesterday the United States of America was suddenly and deliberately attacked by the forces of Imperial Japan; therefore, I declare that a state of war exists between the U.S. and Japan," and ended the declaration with the words "and we shall win the ultimate victory so help us God." It was wonderful how our nation came together and politics were put aside and everyone rallied around the President. Congress passed the declaration of war with one dissenting vote. The next week this prayer for the President appeared in the newspapers across America (author unknown):

> Oh Thou Great Sovereign of all nations, King of Kings and Lord of hosts, in these perilous times of wars and rumors of wars, when all of the powers of hate have been loosed to kill and destroy, we pray Thy Spirit may steady the minds and quicken the hearts of those who call themselves by Thy name. We pray especially for the President of these United States upon whom has been laid heavy burdens and grave responsibilities. Renew his strength for his daily burdens. Give him wisdom and understanding that comes from above. Protect him from those whose methods and motives are preempted by the spirit of selfishness or personal ambition. May he go forth in the consciousness of having fulfilled the task committed to him. And we pray that he with us, shall seek all things that will honor and glorify Thee, hastening the coming of Thy kingdom upon earth—and that the spirit of brotherhood will exist in the minds and hearts of all people on earth so that all nations and peoples may dwell together again in peace and unity. Amen.

To those of us in high school at that time, the joyous mood of the Christmas season turned bleak as we were shocked into the reality of what had happened. As we continued to practice our annual minstrel program to be presented December 10, there was much discussion about canceling the program. But school leaders

President F.D.R. at joint session of Congress declared war on Japan, December 8, 1941.

finally decided to present the program as scheduled because they believed it would be good for the morale of the students and townspeople. Even the elementary children continued with their Christmas programs.

## WAR DECLARED—MEANING OF CHRISTMAS RECOVERED

As the Christmas season continued, Rowan Countians began to recover the real meaning of Christmas. For example, the Girl Scouts initiated a toy collection drive, which is among the ghosts of Christmas 1941, remembered by many Rowan Countians. The Morehead Merchants Club sponsored the event, and the young girls, under the direction of Mrs. W.H. Rice, collected the toys. Broken toys were repaired and distributed by the Agriculture Club, under the direction of Professor H.C. Haggan. Rowan County was still mired in a depression, and Professor Haggan estimated half of the children in Rowan County would not get any toys for Christmas, except for the toy drive. The Morehead Men's Club and the Morehead Merchants Club also met jointly that month and voted $25 to purchase new toys for needy Rowan County Children.

Letters from servicemen also changed the spirit of Christmas in Morehead. Mrs. Flora Hicks received a letter from her son, Pfc. Roy Hicks, who was stationed in Hawaii. At that time, he was enjoying his army experience in a peaceful setting. He was complaining about

Christmas 1941, Uncle Sam as Santa Claus brings good things to our Allies and bombs and bad things to our enemies.

the boredom of being on "alert" 24 hours a day. Unfortunately, they were taken off of "alert" one day before the Japanese attacked on December 7, 1941.

By December 15, 1941, the mood of Moreheadians had changed from joy to sadness, and then back to joy. As Christmas approached, their mood also changed from secular to spiritual, in hope that someday everyone might live in peace, even though the world was at war at the time.

## CHRISTMAS PROGRAMS PRESENTED BY CIVIC AND CHURCH GROUPS

There was an editorial in The Morehead Independent that urged Rowan Countians to "Look up unto the hills for their strength during these troubled times." It was further suggested that Rowan Countians might want to go up to the top of Triangle tower and experience the full meaning of receiving help from the hills.

That was especially good advice for those young men who would soon be leaving the serenity of these hills and might never see them again. That year "The Messiah" was presented by the Morehead Civic Chorus, under the direction of music professor Lewis Henry Horton, for the fifth consecutive year. The Civic Chorus was made up of MSC faculty, students and townspeople. It was an inspired performance that lifted the spirits of all who attended.

During the Christmas season of 1941, the First Church of God presented a program at the church on Sunday evening. That program included Junior Alfrey playing "Under the Stars" on piano, the welcome by Pauline McBrayer and a prayer by James Lowell Ellington. Others on the program included Jack McBrayer, Phyllis Ann Alfrey, Sandra Day and Harold Gee.

Professor H.C. Haggan, Chairman of the local Red Cross, issued an appeal for funds. He predicted there would soon be great demands upon that organization. That appeal raised $2,500 in Rowan County. Those giving $1 or more had their name printed in the paper.

## THEATERS SHOW NEWSREELS OF PEARL HARBOR BOMBING

Many Moreheadians were trying to forget the bloodshed and war around the world by going to the Trail or Mills Theaters. Movies shown that week were "Shepherd of the Hills," starring John Wayne, Harry Carey and Betty Field. In addition, "The March of Time" newsreels promised the latest war news and films of the bombing of Pearl Harbor.

Moreheadians were also listening to Nat King Cole singing "Straighten Up and Fly Right" and Helen Forrest, vocalist for Harry James and the Music Makers, singing "I've Heard That Song Before."

## MERCHANTS OFFER PRE-CHRISTMAS BARGAINS

That year, Allie Jane's Beauty Shoppe offered permanents for $2 and up. A.B. McKinney's Department Store offered men's dress shirts for 59 cents and galoshes for $1. Women's skirts were $1 and step-ins were 50 cents.

*1941*

### The IDEAL CHRISTMAS GIFT
GIVE YOUR LOVED ONES A GIFT THAT THEY WILL USE AND APPRECIATE EVERY DAY NEXT YEAR

Automobiles were cheap. Just one week before Pearl Harbor, my father bought a new 1941 Chevrolet for $540. It had a heater, but no radio. (Every day during WWII someone tried to buy that car from him because no new cars were built until the war ended.)

That year the Kroger grocery store at Main and North Wilson

Avenue offered coffee at three pounds for 53 cents, 100 pounds of potatoes for $1.89 and 25 pounds of Domino sugar for $1.49.

Goldes Department Store offered men's suits and topcoats for $9.98, boys' hi-top leather boots for $1.98 and all wool sweaters for 98 cents. If these all sound like good prices, remember tobacco averaged selling for $29.93 per hundred.

The whole community continued to be in a pensive mood especially when Morehead State College President, Dr. William H. Vaughn, called a special campus convocation and invited the townspeople. He quietly urged the faculty, staff, students and the community to remain calm in this grave crisis facing our nation. He emphasized that "America needed clear thinking and wise citizens." He said, "This is not the hour for emotional hysterics, but a time for everyone to continue the work they are doing until called to other active fields of service." Dr. Vaughn emphasized that Morehead College was ready with its facilities to help in this grave emergency. The Red Cross already had a room on campus and other space would be provided as needed. He stated that "Education is Defense and the American soldier is the best educated soldier in the world." President Vaughn predicted a long war, but said, "Victory will be ours because

CHRISTMAS 1941

## SANTA CLAUS IN ALL HIS GLORY

We Have No Foolishness for Christmas Presents, but We Do Have Presents that are Useful and Ones That Will Be Remembered Long Months After Christmas Is Gone

### See Our Window Display And Be

### Convinced that we can supply you. .

Jewelry, Clocks, Ties, Handkerchief Sets, Belts, Sweaters

Cannon Towels —:— It would take too long to mention All

# THE BIG STORE

A No Foolishness Christmas.

we believe in freedom and justice for all." It was a timely, inspiring and reassuring speech to all who were there.

## CIVIL DEFENSE ORGANIZED AS MEN ENTER THE MILITARY

Many local men had already been drafted into the military service in the summer of 1941. Some were already in battle in the Pacific area. And everyone knew many others would also soon be in harm's way. Among those local men to enter service soon after Pearl Harbor were Robert Brigham Hogge, Claude Dillon Kessler, Walter Carr, Elijah Hogge, Ligon Kessler, Pete Kessler and many more. On the home front during Christmas 1941, Civil Defense programs were organized. Morehead Fire Chief C.B. McCullough was chairman of the County Civil Defense. Eight members made up a board that administered the Civil Defense program.

That board consisted of Boyd McCullough, fire services; Bill Carter, police services; Dr. W.A. Adkins, medical services; Burl Fouch, road services; W.H. Rice, utility services; W.E. "Snooks" Crutcher, public relations; Roy E. Cornette, educational services; and the Rev. A.E. Landolt, church services.

## CASUALTIES LISTED—MEN JOIN THE MILITARY

The war became personal when Irvin Hamm, son of Mr. and Mrs. Melvin Hamm of Morehead, was listed as the first local casualty of WWII. On December 10, his parents received the following message, "The Navy Department deeply regrets to inform you that your son, Willie Irvin Hamm, Coxswain, U.S.N., has been wounded in action in the performance of his duty in the service of his country. The Department greatly appreciates your anxiety and will furnish you with additional information when received. Signed Rear Admiral Chester Nimitz." To prevent aid to the enemy, he did not divulge

Coxswain W. Irvin Hamm wounded at Pearl Harbor. He survived.

the name of the ship or its base (which was Pearl Harbor). Everyone at school remembered Irvin and we suddenly had a personal interest because he was the first casualty of WWII from Rowan County.

Rowan County and Eastern Kentucky residents quickly responded to the call of their country for additional men to join the military forces of this nation. Dozens joined in a few days including J.T. Daugherty who had already entered the Naval Air Corp on December 2. He went on to become a Marine pilot and a hero in the Pacific theater. He later was in the first class of Astronauts this country had and one of the subjects of my book, *Patriots & Heroes, Eastern Kentucky Soldiers of WWII.* Another early Morehead resident who enlisted in the Navy was seventeen year old Robert Brigmon Hogge, son of Mrs. Mary Hogge of Morehead. He arrived at the Naval Training Base at Great Lake, Illinois, on December 11. On December 12, Colonel E.R. Pierson, this nation's Fifth Corps Recruiting Officer, announced the need for 320 men in the Air Corps immediately. These men were to come from Kentucky, Indiana, Ohio and West Virginia. Age limits were 18 - 35 and the men would be shipped to Kessler Field in Biloxi, Mississippi, for basic training. (That's where I was assigned three years later.) It was announced that 550 auto mechanics from defense industries were urgently needed to be trained as aircraft mechanics. All who entered

WWII were in for the duration of the war plus six months. Of course "The Duration" was unknown but it would seem like "a lifetime plus six months" to the 16 million men who would take the oath that swept them into WWII.

## OATH OF ENLISTMENT INTO THE US MILITARY SERVICE 1789 - 1960

The first oath under the constitution was approved by Act of Congress 29 September 1789 (Sec. 3, Ch. 25, 1st Congress). For enlisted soldiers, the oath did not change until 1960. It came in two parts, the first of which read:

> I (your name) do solemnly swear or affirm that I will support and defend the constitution of the United States against all enemies both foreign and domestic. I also do solemnly swear or affirm to bear true allegiance to the United States of America, and to serve honestly and faithfully against all their enemies both foreign and domestic, or opposers whatsoever, and to observe and obey the orders of the President of the United States of America, and the orders of the officers appointed over me, so help me God.

## CHRISTMAS BELLS RANG IN AMERICA: SILENT AROUND THE WORLD

The world was at war before Christmas, 1941, and it appeared that the joyous Christmas bells would be silent around the world. During Christmas 1941, one month from my fifteenth birthday, I had a paper route delivering the Lexington *Leader* in my hometown. I was able to follow the progress of the war through the eyes of that newspaper. I recall there was not much joy in our town or our nation. As I delivered my papers each evening during that first wartime

# "Christmas under Fire"
## England 1940

The short propaganda film, *Christmas under Fire*, made by England's Ministry of Information, was shown in theaters in 1941. The film depicts how Christmas was celebrated in that island nation during the war in 1940. The movie—which can be seen on YouTube.com—offers a touching portrait of holiday preparations in war-torn London and other parts of the country. The movie shows choirs rehearsing Christmas carols and parents buying toys for their children. Scenes of little boys playing soldier and little girls playing nurse illustrate the kinds of toys the children wanted for Christmas. Taking pride in their ability to identify war planes, to tell a Spitfire from a Messerschmitt, for instance, some of them asked for model airplanes. Christmas trees are set up in family living rooms. Trees are even decorated and set up in the underground railroad stations that served as bomb shelters for Londoners. Though no church bells rang out on Christmas Eve, because church bells were used as warnings of enemy invasion, Christmas was still celebrated. Propaganda though it is, the film convincingly claims what history has confirmed: the strong spirit and determination of the English people during World War II. As the movie narrator says, Christmas in England during the war was strange, "a Christmas of contrasts: holly and barbed wire, guns and tinsel," but it was all the more Christmas because of the many hardships, the shared danger, and the dearly held hope for peace.

Christmas season, I would hear the local churches' Christmas bells ring out the familiar refrain: "I heard the bells on Christmas day, their old familiar carols play, and wild and sweet, the words repeat, of peace on earth, good will to men."

It seemed from the terrible war news around the world that only on our land did the bells ring out freely in joyous song that Christmas of 1941. All across this continent that year the sound of ringing bells celebrated that great holiday which for centuries had brought joy and gladness to all people even to the humblest homes.

The Christmas bells of Germany that once rang out during the Christmas season were silent in 1941. Instead of the beautiful strains of "Oh, Tannenbaum," Germany blared military music in defiance of the wisdom of the Prince of Peace.

The bells of Austria were also mute. The lovely "Stille Nacht," written by a parish priest for his faithful flock, was mute that Christmas. Austria had been crushed and had little heart to sing. The carillons of Belgium, which usually rang from their tall belfries, had been stilled, and there was little hope in Holland that year that Kris Kringle would appear with his bag of toys for good children.

The hauntingly exquisite "Noel, Noel," that sweet carol beloved of all Christmas songs, did not ring through a France saddened, torn by war and an even more devastating peace. In 1941, France was threatened both within and without by new occupation and Nazi tyranny. Russia's Christmas bells, long mute for all practical purposes, had been silenced. The bells of Italy, what could they mean this year to women left at home as their men died in aggression against peaceful neighbors? What could the grand motif of "Adeste Fideles" mean to a nation locked in an unholy alliance with Nazi Germany?

In England bells sent children scurrying to underground air raid shelters, not to happy gatherings. Many children were sent out of the cities and away from their parents to the greater safety of the countryside.

And yet, the Christmas bells, in our land were still free. As the bells of Christmas resounded in this writer's "Old Kentucky Home" and throughout our nation that Christmas of 1941, they offered a hope for the world. For only in America did those Christmas bells ringing revive the hope of the world, especially in those lands where the Christmas joy was dimmed by the ravages of war. That memorable year those old familiar tunes offered a hope of joy to the world and a time of peace on earth and good will to all just as it had on that first Christmas 1941 years earlier.

# WORLD WAR II
## ALLIES & AXIS NATIONS
### 1942 - 1946

---

### ALLIES

| | |
|---|---|
| 1. U.S. | 16. Dominican Republic |
| 2. Great Britain | 17. El Salvador |
| 3. China | 18. Ethiopia |
| 4. Russia | 19. Free France |
| 5. Canada | 20. Greece |
| 6. Australia | 21. Norway |
| 7. Belgium | 22. Philippines |
| 8. India | 23. Poland |
| 9. Mexico | 24. South Africa |
| 10. Netherlands | 25. Yugoslavia |
| 11. Panama | 26. Haiti |
| 12. Brazil | 27. Honduras |
| 13. Costa Rica | 28. Luxemburg |
| 14. Cuba | 29. Nicaragua |
| 15. Czechoslovakia | 30. Guatemala |

### AXIS

| | |
|---|---|
| 1. Germany | 6. Hungary |
| 2. Italy | 7. Romania |
| 3. Japan | 8. Slovakia |
| 4. France (Occupied) | 9. Thailand |
| 5. Finland | 10. Croatia |
| 11. Bulgaria | |

1944 High School graduates: (left to right) Jack Ellis, Bob Ramey, Frank Burns, Bill Bradley, and Meredith Mynhier. All served in WWII except Bob Ramey.

## CHAPTER 4
# School "Daze:" War Years

"The heart of him with understanding seeketh knowledge."
(Proverbs 15:14)

Those of us who were high school students during the early dark days of WWII were confronted with bewildering decisions never before faced by the youth of America. The worldwide conflict produced so many problems it was difficult to decide even what classes we should take in order to best prepare ourselves for an uncertain future. We wondered whether we should even remain in high school knowing that on our 18th birthday we would be called upon to defend our country in a battle for survival. Should we just have a good time while we could? With the list of war casualties coming in every week, there was the haunting question in the back of every high school boy's mind: "What if you are one of the KIA (killed in action) and don't make it back?"

We wondered whether we should quit school and get a job on a farm or in a defense plant. We could get a job on a farm, which was considered essential to the war effort, and be exempt from military service entirely, but I don't believe any of the boys in my high school graduating class of 1944 even thought of shirking his patriotic duty.

Many even volunteered before finishing high school. I was one of those who volunteered while in high school but was permitted to graduate before being called into active duty.

## HIGH SCHOOL SPORTS CURTAILED

In 1942 - 43 Morehead High School had two separate basketball coaches. At the beginning of the year Richard "Feets" Daugherty was our coach. Basketball was the only sport in our high school during the war. But Coach Daugherty was drafted. He was soon replaced by "Moose" Zachem, who finished the basketball season before being drafted. Both were popular Morehead College athletes who

Morehead High School Vikings Basketball Players: (left to right, front row) Bill Bradley, Frank Burns, James Hall, Jack Ellis (Captain), Berkely Cox, Quentin Hicks; (back row) Bob Stamper (Manager), Freeman Spencer, Clyde Day, Ralph Christian, Richard Maxey, Roy Stewart and Coach Telford Gevedon. Four seniors: Bradley, Burns, Hall and Ellis.

coached on a part-time basis and were paid $40 per month. Biology teacher Telford Gevedon was listed as Athletic Director and his supplemental salary for that job was $20 per month. The next year, Telford Gevedon (too old to be drafted) was both coach and Athletic Director. It was difficult to keep the school open and maintain any kind of sports program during WWII, but the limited programs were continued on a limited basis. Our basketball team never knew who would be on the team each game because many players were drafted into the Army before finishing high school. Many games were played in the afternoon because travel at night was difficult.

**BLACKOUTS AND AIRCRAFT SPOTTERS**

On July 16, 1942, Moreheadians were brought to the stark reality of war when the local City Council unanimously enacted a "Blackout Ordinance." According to C.B. McCullough, Chairman of Civil Defense in Rowan County, its purpose was to regulate blackouts in the city. It was met with skepticism by those of us in high school. First of all, it limited our going out later at night, and secondly, we questioned whether Morehead really was in danger of an air attack. Also, then if you were home at night, you had to make sure your curtains and shades were closed tightly so that no light could be observed around the edge of your windows. Civil Defense Chairman McCullough said he realized there was little chance Morehead would suffer an air raid; however, all cities in Kentucky were asked to adopt such an ordinance and be prepared for all emergencies.

There were several schools in our region that adopted a program of "Air Craft Spotters." That was when many of us as young teenagers were given a pair of binoculars and we took turns as Aircraft Spotters. As a part of a class called "Aeronautics" in high school, we learned to identify various American aircraft, as well as enemy

Liberty Bell—Symbol of Freedom was motivation for war bond drives.

aircraft. We were given photos and silhouettes of different Japanese and German airplanes which we studied faithfully. Soon we were able to distinguish between a German ME 100 and an American P51. Needless to say, we never spotted any enemy aircraft, and probably never spotted any aircraft at all. But it gave everyone a sense of being a part of the war effort.

All citizens prepared to assist the war effort, and there was not too much grumbling. Also, the ordinance had plenty of teeth. It called for fines up to $500 and imprisonment for not more than six months for failure to observe all regulations. There were volunteer "blackout" wardens in each neighborhood assigned to check to make sure the regulations were being observed. So far as I remember no one was ever cited for that infraction during WWII.

## NEW CLASSES OFFERED TO STUDENTS

During my senior year, when I took "Aeronautics," I was fascinated with the subject. Even though the teacher had never been in an airplane, her class was probably one of the reasons I later joined the Army Air Corps. There were guest speakers, and on one occasion, Air Cadet James Butcher was home on leave and told us of his experiences learning to fly. He still tells me about a question I asked him that day that he couldn't answer. He can't remember the answer and I sure can't remember the question.

In early 1943, Defense Rural War Production classes began in earnest in Rowan County schools. One of those classes included two phases of education in order to receive maximum benefits from farm

County Agent, Adrian Razor (standing) talks to a group of farmers as well as Morehead State College Professor Haggan (seated front), teaching better farm production methods.

production. Those were classes in repairing farm machinery, since no new machinery was available because of the war. Also, there were different classes on how to increase production in poultry, eggs, pork, beef and vegetables. Other county schools in Elliottville and Sharkey were more interested in the farm machinery repair classes. Haldeman taught adult classes on better farm production. Slab Camp, Upper Lick Fork and Perkins taught five classes for adults in better farm production.

The war years (1941 - 1945) were a time of turmoil and trauma in the Rowan County schools. Sixteen-year-old boys and girls could go north and get a job in a war plant making more money than teachers were being paid. Seventeen and 18-year-old boys were drafted (or volunteered) into the military. Girls 16 - 18 went away to work in defense plants. In 1940, 140 freshmen enrolled in Morehead High School and only 22 graduated in 1944. Many teachers resigned to work in the war industries or to enter military service.

Food, clothing, gasoline, coal, electricity, tires, and many others things were rationed. There was a shortage of paper ink and school supplies. There were no school newspapers or yearbooks printed. Clubs and other activities were curtailed. Very few school plays were produced. Boys' basketball was the only sport that continued during those years. Many games were played in the afternoon and only 10 boys traveled in taxis to their away games (taxis could get gasoline). The four cheerleaders were transported by parents who saved their gasoline stamps. There was very little record of any high school activities during those years. When boys who would have been playing high school sports were dying in battle, sports didn't seem that important in the total scheme of things.

**WWII BROUGHT SHORTAGES OF TEACHERS, FUEL AND SUPPLIES**

It was difficult to get enough teachers during those years. However, high school graduates were issued emergency certificates to teach in Rowan schools. Retired teachers and former teachers came

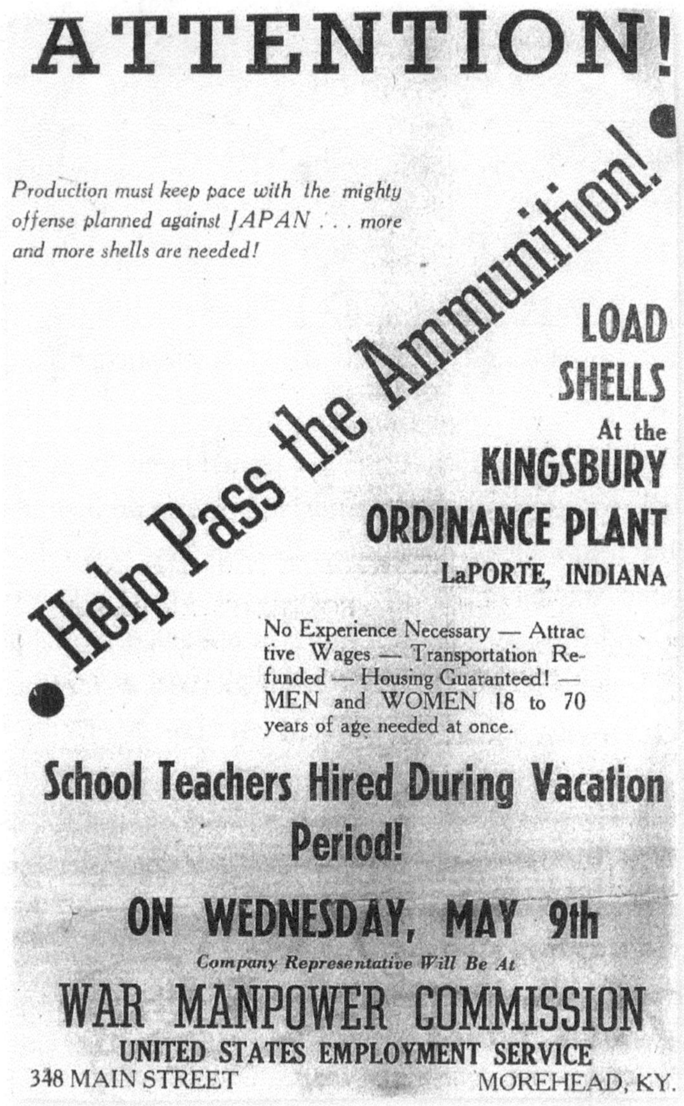

# ATTENTION!

*Production must keep pace with the mighty offense planned against JAPAN . . . more and more shells are needed!*

Help Pass the Ammunition!

LOAD
SHELLS
At the
KINGSBURY
ORDINANCE PLANT
LaPORTE, INDIANA

No Experience Necessary — Attractive Wages — Transportation Refunded — Housing Guaranteed! — MEN and WOMEN 18 to 70 years of age needed at once.

**School Teachers Hired During Vacation Period!**

## ON WEDNESDAY, MAY 9th

*Company Representative Will Be At*

# WAR MANPOWER COMMISSION

UNITED STATES EMPLOYMENT SERVICE

348 MAIN STREET       MOREHEAD, KY.

Students walk a muddy road to get to their rural one-room school (Old House Creek).

back to the classroom. Each teacher accepted larger class sizes, and the schools were kept open. Transportation was a problem then as it is now. But the problems were different. Then there was a shortage of buses (none were manufactured). Also, there was a shortage of parts, gasoline, and tires, as well as a shortage of skilled mechanics. The Office of Defense Transportation surveyed every school bus route in Rowan County, and examined all school bus engines in Rowan County for greater efficiency. Gasoline was rationed, and with a fuel shortage, one way of increasing efficiency was fewer school bus stops. Therefore, the buses stopped every two miles on the route instead of every mile. That meant that some children, even though they lived directly on the route, could still have to walk one mile to catch the school bus. But if they did not live directly on the route, they had to walk even farther. (It's no wonder there were fewer obese children in WWII.) Since there were fewer stops, fuel efficiency was increased.

The gasoline saved by children walking farther was one way of helping the war effort. No one really complained because the buses did keep running during the war years.

Allen, Edison, and Henry Clay McKinney on their way to rural one-room school during WWII. (Henry Clay was killed in the Korean War.)

Another problem in those days was the shortage of coal needed to heat the schools. Getting enough coal to the schools was a logistical as well as a supply problem. There was a great interest shown by many people when the bids for the schools' coal contracts were opened. It was one of the major school expenses every year, and many people attended those bid openings.

## FOLLOWING THE MONEY TRAIL

Recently I came into possession of an old book of check stubs from the Rowan County Board of Education. There were 596 check stubs dated December 19, 1942 through March 26, 1943. That public document could have legally been destroyed many years ago, but it has somehow survived these 60 years, and as an old historian who was a junior at Morehead High School that year, I am thankful it did survive. That document gave me a sense of the priorities of that school system. My mother was a teacher in the Rowan County schools that year and was the recipient of some of those checks. Also, the checks were written in the familiar handwriting of my wife's mother (Myrtle Caudill). She was the business manager for the school board, and Roy Cornette was the superintendent who signed the checks. Those canceled checks give one a clear insight of the very primitive condition of the schools in Rowan County during the dark days of WWII.

The first check dated December 19, 1942 in the amount of $13.50 was paid to Willie Brown for 34 hours labor and materials for repairing a leaky roof on a one-room school. Teachers who made the "big bucks" in December 1942, included Verner Tackett, $72.07; Beulah Williams, $83.61; Elizabeth Layne, three days substitute, $12.93; and Mary Patrick was paid $32.40 for eight days substituting.

Bus drivers in 1942 included B.W. Moore, Emory Butler, Sherman Conn, Elmer Plank and John Kelly. The average salary was $35.00 per month. John Bashford was paid $9 for two months of building fires in the bus garage. He furnished his own kindling. The Williams-Nickell Oil Company was paid $123.22 for gasoline for school buses for the month of December. W.H. Bradley, who was a teacher in Rowan County schools, had taken a job as janitor at Morehead High School. His salary of $85 was considerably more than he would have made as a teacher.

## VICTORY TAX FOR WWII

The first check written in January 1, 1943, was to my mother, Dorothy Ellis, in the amount of $64.75. It was for the month of December (less five days). Also for the first time there were deductions for the new "Victory Tax." It was an additional tax, placed on everyone, to help pay for the war. I never heard anyone complain about the "Victory Tax" during WWII because everyone wanted to do their part and believed it was necessary to win the war.

FORM AC-CP-60
REVISED 3-23-43

eiw

## WAR DEPARTMENT
## ARMY AIR FORCES

Date: Nov. 15, 1943

NOTIFICATION OF PERSONNEL ACTION

Patterson Field
*Station*

Fairfield, Ohio
*Location*

*FATHER OF
JACK ELLIS*

This is to notify you of the following action concerning your employment:

1. TO: __Lon__ __B.__ __Ellis__
   *First Name*      *Middle Initial*      *Last Name*

2. Through: __Supply__
   *Office in which employed or to be employed*

3. Nature of action: __Res. (Vol.)__
   *Use standard terminology*

4. Effective date: __Nov. 15, 1943__

| | FROM | TO |
|---|---|---|
| 5. Position | Carpenter | |
| 6. Salary | $2200 per annum | |
| 7. Grade | Ungraded | |
| 8. Activity | Army Air Forces | |
| 9. Duty Station | Fairfield Air Depot Patterson Field Fairfield, Ohio FIELD | FIELD |

10. Remarks: To return home to take care of farm.

Form 3005 forwarded to Retirement Office, Headquarters, Army Air Forces.

This action is subject to the provisions on the reverse hereof, when applicable.

For the Commanding Officer

*Civilian Personnel Officer*

R. D. PENLAND, Lt. Col., Air Corps,
Chief, Civilian Personnel Section.

*(This information to be furnished only in "S. Trans." cases.)*

11. The records of this station show that the leave status of this individual
as of_____was as follows:

| | Total accumulated and accrued | | | Overdrawn | | |
|---|---|---|---|---|---|---|
| Annual | ____Da. | ____Hr. | ____Min. | ____Da. | ____Hr. | ____Min. |
| Sick | ____Da. | ____Hr. | ____Min. | ____Da. | ____Hr. | ____Min. |

MANIFOLD
INTERLEAVED PATO-GILMAN FANFOLD CORP. NIAGARA FALLS N.Y.

EMPLOYEE'S COPY

War Department Defense Plant work record—Lon Ellis.

It was amazing to me how that one check stub for my mother's paycheck brought back so many memories. I remembered that the reason my mother missed five days' teaching during December 1942 was because she had gone to visit my Dad, who was a carpenter working for the War Department in Fairfield, Ohio, helping to build that military base. When my mother reached my Dad's apartment in Fairfield, Ohio, she said his landlady asked to see her marriage license. Of course she did not have it with her, and the landlady wouldn't let her in until my Dad came in from work that day.

After my mother purchased her ticket on the train to visit my Dad, I asked her to leave her car keys with me since I had just learned to drive. Of course, she refused, saying she was taking the keys with her. It was then I found an old car key which, before my mother left, I secretly switched for the ignition key to our new 1941 Chevrolet five-passenger coupe. I drove the car a couple of times that week, scared to death I would have an accident. When she returned and tossed the keys to me and said to back the car out of the garage, it had no trouble switching the key back. It was not until I returned from the Army that I confessed to her what I had done.

### ADVANTAGES AND DISADVANTAGES OF THE WAR YEARS

Those of us attending high school during WWII had both advantages and disadvantages over previous students. Because of the war, the Great Depression had ended, and there were many more opportunities for students to work in defense plants where men were urgently needed. I spent my sixteenth summer, after finishing my third year of high school, working in a defense plant in Dayton, Ohio. I was cutting parachute webbing in a parachute factory. (Little did I realize that I might be wearing one of those parachutes during my time in the 32nd Troop Carrier Squadron in Europe in 1945 - 46.)

# "When the Lights Go On Again"

There is a recent song which runs like this "When the lights come on again all over the world." Some of us are living for that time. We are looking forward eagerly to that day, but there are some things that we can see in the dark better than in the light. Owls can see better at night than by day and that is also true of people concerning some lessons that we need to learn.

Maybe that is one reason the lights have gone off all over the world, to teach us to see things we did not see when they were on, and above all to see God. Isaiah said, "I saw the Lord." That is a great experience in the life of any individual or nation. A lot of people see everything else but God.

It is to be hoped that when the lights come on again our people will have God in His proper place in their lives and that we will realize what we have seemed blind to before— that a world wrong toward God can not be right anywhere; that Christ in the hearts of men is all that can prevent a spiritual blackout; that is all, also, that can cause men to dwell together in unity and peace.

If we do not learn this lesson and put the lesson hence-forth where it belongs, both for ourselves and for the world, this experience of war conditions will have been in vain both from our standpoint and God's. He has a purpose running through the ages and through each of our lives. It runs sometimes in the dark, as is the case now, but is not broken.

God grant that the time through which we are passing will not be found to have been in vain, but that we will come forth from the crucible of suffering purged, like gold, of the dross and with a new dedication of heart and life to Christ, and a new resolve to spend ourselves in advancing His kingdom—Bell Ave. Baptist Bulletin, Knoxville, Tenn.

Also, while working that summer in Dayton, I became close friends with Joe (I don't remember his last name). He was awaiting his call into the Army. Joe used to sing at the top of his lungs while he was

working, "When the lights go on again all over the world." I never saw Joe again after that summer in Dayton, Ohio. But in Germany in 1945, I met a mutual friend who told me Joe was killed in the Battle of the Bulge. Unfortunately, Joe did not live to see "the lights go on again all over the world." At the end of my summer job, I wanted to remain there because I was making more money than my mother was making teaching school. But being a schoolteacher, my mother told me firmly that was not going to happen. I returned to Kentucky and finished high school before entering the service.

The war created more opportunities for girls and women, who were in great demand as bookkeepers, stenographers, and salespeople. The government and industry needed workers immediately. Because of the war there was also a great demand for nurses—for both army and civilian service. In those programs the standards had also been lowered and girls could then take nurse's training without college work. Also, WWII created more demand for social workers, Salvation Army, Red Cross, U.S.O., and civilian defense workers. Because men were being called into military service, women for the first time were working in defense plants at high salaries. Many became electrical workers, carpenters, welders, airplane mechanics, and filling station operators. Some of those jobs required only a high school education and others required a short course for preparation and training.

Immediate employment and high salaries for high school graduates provided a strong argument against further education. The requirements of age and efficiency had been lowered and we could meet the requirements for those positions immediately. But those decisions were always made in light of the absolute certainty we would soon be entering that major conflict called WWII—and any decision was temporary. However, there were post war problems to consider. With millions of men and women returning from the war it would be very difficult for those who dropped out of high school to obtain employment. Standards of employment would be raised again and we would need to be better educated to be able to get a job.

# Riveters, Pilots, & Nurses

During World War II, Millions of men enrolled in the military leaving their old jobs vacant. In addition, the war effort needed more than soldiers. Overall, there was more work to be done than men to do the work. The shortage of workers offered greater opportunities for women than ever before. In civilian life, "Rosie the Riveter" exemplified the hard-working, high-spirited women who took on jobs at home to support the war abroad. Though the original Rosie may have been modeled on Rose Will Monroe, from Pulaski County, Kentucky, images of "Rosie," appeared over and over again in various forms, such as the red-haired young woman drawn by Norman Rockwell for the May 29, 1943, cover of the *Saturday Evening Post* and on the woman flexing her bicep on the "We Can Do It" poster that is still popular today. Though at that time, women were not allowed on the battlefield to fight, they did take on supportive quasi-military roles. Thousands of women pilots ferried airplanes from one place to another, thus freeing thousands of male pilots for fighter and bombing missions over Europe and the islands of the Pacific. Women became official members of the US armed services during World War II. The establishment of women's service corps—the Navy's WAVE (Women Accepted for Volunteer Emergency Service) in 1942, the Army's WAC (Women Army Corps) in 1943, and the WASP (Women's Air Force Service Pilots) in 1943—reflected the essential nature of women's roles in the war. Women pilots ferried military planes from near their manufacturers to points of departure for Europe or the Pacific. These women freed thousands of male pilots for combat. Though women didn't enter the war as soldiers, their support roles sometimes took them into combat zones. Nurses working at hospitals on the battlefront often came under fire. In a *Now & Then* article on Appalachian veterans, author Pat Arnow quotes veteran Army nurse Pearl Quillen, who did her nurse's training in Abingdon, Virginia. After Pearl joined the Army, she landed in Anzio, Italy. Quillen said that when they landed, "Shrapnel was falling. It was red-hot." While working there at the 15th Evacuation Hospital, Pearl, along with other medical staff, helped dig foxholes, sandbagged, and lived in foxholes during three months of almost constant artillery fire. For Quillen and thousands of other women, life would never be the same.

One hundred forty four freshmen at Morehead High School in 1940, only twenty graduated in 1944. (Left to right) first row: Grace Crosthwaite (teacher), Arlene McClain, Olive Jent, Iris Hutchinson, Lily Mae Hamilton; second row: Verna Johnson, Gloria Carpenter, Juanita Maxey, Margie Stewart; third row: Jack Ellis, Thelma Roe, Virginia Amburgey; fourth row: Bill Bradley, Aurola Kegley, James Hall, Pauline Binion; fifth row: Carl Lewis, Frank Burns, Milford Ellington.

Those of us in high school during WWII always seemed to realize that many changes and adjustments would have to be made in our lives because of the war. However, we realized that after we won the war (and we never doubted we would win), and if we survived, we would have to be prepared for a post WWII America. Those graduating during the years of WWII had an advantage over the graduates of the pre-war years. There were many opportunities open to us. We could start right into work in a defense plant, where men were so badly needed. There was a place for carpenters, machinists, electric welders, and mechanics. In fact, there was a place for everyone who knew a trade or was capable of learning quickly.

During WWII it was extremely necessary to increase our country's agricultural output. Those graduating who lived on farms intended to make that happen. Those who had been taking Agriculture for four years knew more about new farming methods their fathers had not learned in all their year of farming experience.

## BE DRAFTED OR VOLUNTEER—THAT WAS THE QUESTION

In high school it seemed odd to hear some of the older boys talking about receiving and filling out their questionnaires to be drafted into the Army. And, as a result of those draft notices being received by 18-year-old boys, I asked several of them this question: "How do you feel about the 18-year draft law?" Each had the same unselfish answer saying in no uncertain terms, "We think that boys of 18 should be taken first into the Army, Navy, or any branch of the service where they are best suited and most needed. If younger men are not drafted, the men of 40 and 45 would have to be taken away from vital jobs and their families. It is a well known fact that boys of this age are in better physical condition to become soldiers than older men. They have more stamina and can stand higher altitudes

A Service Flag that hung in the Student Center at Morehead State College kept a monthly total of former students. By May, 1942, 536 had enlisted in Military Service, with 6 killed in action.

in airplanes and are much more likely to recover from wounds." That is why I call us the "Unselfish Generation."

But most of us felt that those in high school should be allowed to finish their last year of high school before being taken into the Army.

I asked one boy this question: "How do you feel about going into the armed forces?" He answered simply and in a manner that reflected his youth, "I can hardly wait until I am in some phase of the armed forces so that I can take a crack at a Jap or Nazi. Boy, but I'd like to be in one of the babies which are going to blow Tokyo off the map." Also, one advantage of entering the military was we would be permitted to go to technical schools. Among the things we could train for were airplane mechanics, radio, engineering, and other courses, which would be of tremendous help to us at the time, and after the war was won.

There was also the question of how well the younger soldiers would be able to re-adjust to a civilian way of life. That question could not be answered then, but it was given much consideration. Of course, we all realized that it would be difficult for us to pick up our civilian life just where we left off. We would be older and have the experience of a war fought and won. But most believed it would be easier for younger men to re-adjust than for older men. It seemed to us that if anyone had made plans for the future, they would try to continue them after the war. The experience we gained training, traveling, making decisions, and facing dangers would enable us to be more mature in deciding what we wanted to do after the war was won.

But whatever we did, we wanted to remember that these problems must be met if we were to defend the American principles for which we were fighting a war. But with the aid and advice of our parents and teachers, and with our faith in God, we believed we would be successful in surviving the war and re-adjusting to civilian life. One thing was sure that each one of us realized that WWII had to be won first, and then if we survived, we could face the post-war era with confidence and faith in the future. Ah, the eternal optimism of youth! (The older veterans had the most readjustment problems.)

War Rationing Boards established January, 1942. *Photo: National Archives.*

## CHAPTER 5

# Rationing on the Home Front

"Gather up the fragments that nothing be lost. (John 6:12)

Less than thirty days after the Japanese bombed Pearl Harbor, this nation began to mobilize—not just men, machines, and war materials for the battlefront, but resources for the home front. Rationing was instituted for the purpose of distributing goods equally between the rich and the poor. It was soon determined that food, clothes, gasoline, rubber, silk, tin, kitchen fats, leather products, and even cigarettes were soon going to be in short supply. In order to eliminate hording, reduce black marketing, and reduce inflation, special price controls were established. Also, a rationing system for those products vital to the war effort that were in short supply, were quickly established. Actually, water, one item not generally known as vital to the war effort, was rationed in Morehead. Each individual was allowed 20 gallons of water a day. That was not because of a drought, but because the water could not be purified fast enough to meet the demand.

On January 11, 1942, a rationing board was established in Kentucky. Governor Keen Johnson met with business and professional leaders from forty-five Eastern Kentucky counties on the campus

GAS RATIONING

# C STICKER – ESSENTIAL ACTIVITIES

- ☐ Official Gov't or Red Cross business.
- ☐ School official traveling school to school.
- ☐ Transportation 4 or more to school.
- ☐ Transportation of United States mail.
- ☐ Wholesale newspaper delivery.
- ☐ Carrying newsreel photographic equipment.
- ☐ Physician, surgeon, veterinarian.
- ☐ Public Health nurse or interne.
- ☐ Embalmer.
- ☐ Minister, priest or rabbi.
- ☐ Transportation of farm workers, marine workers, or farm materials.
- ☐ Essential hospital, utility, or war worker.
- ☐ Labor conciliation, recruiting, training workers.
- ☐ Construction, repair, maintenance services or production specialist.
- ☐ Members of Armed Forces to duty.
- ☐ Telegram delivery.
- ☐ Essential scrap agent.

Any of these activities were issued a "C" Gas Ration Card.

of Morehead State College. Their goal was to establish a three-man War Ration Board (that's what it was called) in each county. There would be one Democrat, one Republican, and one Independent citizen on each Board. The first duty of the War Ration Board was to determine if applicants for rationed products met the national criteria established by the U.S. Office of Price Controls and the national War Rationing Board. Because the U.S. supply of raw rubber from Southeast Asia had been taken over by the Japanese, rubber was the first product to be rationed. It was immediately determined that the first people who would be permitted to purchase automobile tires were health and safety officials, as well as those in industrial and commercial operations. The following criteria were established: (1) Vehicles used by physicians, surgeons, visiting nurses or veterinarians, principally for professional medical personnel and ambulance services; (2) Vehicles used "exclusively" for fire fighting services, necessary public police services, enforcement of specific laws affecting public health and safety, garbage removal or other sanitation services or mail delivery; and (3) Vehicles, buses and taxis, with a capacity of ten or more passengers operated "exclusively" to carry passengers as part of "services rendered to the public."

A "C" sticker displayed on your auto windshield allowed you enough gasoline for your job. A "B" sticker allowed you 8 gallons per week.

By early spring of 1942 War Ration Book Number One was issued to each home in America. Products that were rationed included food

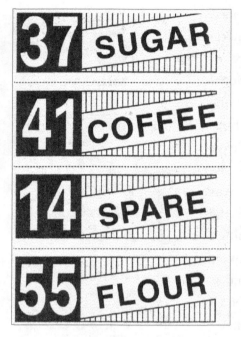

You had to have these stamps to purchase food staples.

(sugar, coffee, meat, canned goods, cooking oils), clothing (leather products, silk products) as well as gasoline, and automobile parts. It was the rationing of gasoline that hurt the most, although cigarettes were also worth their weight in gold. Needless to say there was some black marketing at that time. However, anyone caught was not only heavily fined but was considered un-American and ostracized by almost everyone in the community.

In early 1943, it was time for all Americans to register again for Ration Book Number Two. On February 24 and 25, forty-one teachers volunteered to register Rowan countians for War Ration Book Number Two. In two days they registered over 10,000 individuals (not families). But all members of each family had to be listed with their age and sex given. Registration took place at the following schools: Morehead, Haldeman, Elliottville, Farmers, Clearfield, and Cranston. That complicated task of registering over 10,000 Rowan countians for War Ration Book Number Two went smoothly. No one attempted to cheat on the number of children and adults in their family because it was local teachers doing the registering and they knew each family personally.

Practically every citizen in America participated unselfishly in

828/401 DV

UNITED STATES OF AMERICA
OFFICE OF PRICE ADMINISTRATION

WAR RATION BOOK TWO

IDENTIFICATION

Ellis, John

(Name of person to whom book is issued)

Cogswell      Ky.    62   M   828/401 DV
(Street number or rural route)

(City or post office)      (State)    (Age)   (Sex)

ISSUED BY LOCAL BOARD No. 105   Rowan    Ky.
              (County)        (State)

Main St.      Morehead
(Street address of local board)      (City)

By Grace Cross Everett
(Signature of issuing officer)

SIGNATURE
(To be signed by the person to whom this book is issued. If such person is unable to sign because of age or incapacity, another may sign in his behalf)

OFFICE
OF
PRICE ADM.

**WARNING**

1   This book is the property of the United States Government. It is unlawful to sell or give it to any other person or to use it or permit anyone else to use it, except to obtain rationed goods for the person to whom it was issued.

2   This book must be returned to the War Price and Rationing Board which issued it, if the person to whom it was issued is inducted into the armed services of the United States, or leaves the country for more than 30 days, or dies. The address of the Board appears above.

3   A person who finds a lost War Ration Book must return it to the War Price and Rationing Board which issued it.

4   PERSONS WHO VIOLATE RATIONING REGULATIONS ARE SUBJECT TO $10,000 FINE OR IMPRISONMENT, OR BOTH.

Every home in America had ration books each year for food, clothing, shoes, and other basic necessities.

the rationing process, as well as doing without many things we had previously thought a necessity. To do otherwise was considered unpatriotic, and rationing made everyone feel like they were helping in the war effort. The idea was that, whatever the shortage, we were to make do with what we had. We were expected to use it up, repair it, share it, or recycle it. The word "recycle" was not yet in our vocabulary, but that's exactly what we were doing.

If you had five tires you were expected to turn one back in and do without a spare tire. Since the tires all had rubber inner tubes, if you had a flat tire, you had to patch the inner tube. Also, there were times it was necessary to put a "boot" inside the tire. It was like putting a heavy patch inside the tire. That would make for a rough ride

# *Tire Rationing Boards Of Seventh, Eighth Districts To Meet Here Today At 2 P.M.*

but it gave more life to the tire. All of these methods of conservation gave us greater mileage to each tire. Also, the Caudill brothers' tire recapping business was kept busy helping to keep people moving. Should anyone become weary and complain, you would hear the most used phrase during WWII, "Don't you know there's a war on?"

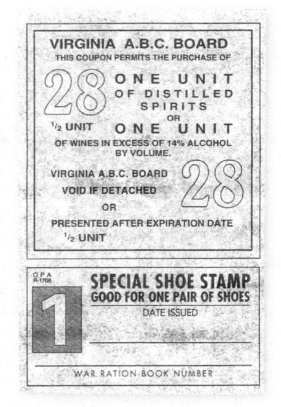

VIRGINIA A.B.C. BOARD
THIS COUPON PERMITS THE PURCHASE OF

28 ONE UNIT OF DISTILLED SPIRITS

OR

½ UNIT ONE UNIT OF WINES IN EXCESS OF 14% ALCOHOL BY VOLUME.

VIRGINIA A.B.C. BOARD VOID IF DETACHED 28 OR PRESENTED AFTER EXPIRATION DATE ½ UNIT

O P A R-1708

1 SPECIAL SHOE STAMP
GOOD FOR ONE PAIR OF SHOES
DATE ISSUED

WAR RATION BOOK NUMBER

Among those who were first required to register for War Ration books were businesses, wholesalers, retailers, and commercial establishments such as grocery stores, gas stations, garages, restaurants, and hotels. All were under strict control based on their past sales.

An "A" card on your windshield permitted you only 3 gallons of gas a week and had nothing to do with your job.

Individual families were registered for their War Ration Books based upon how important their job was to the war effort. Doctors, farmers, defense workers would get more gasoline than others got. But the amount of food was equally distributed based upon the number and ages of the people in the family. I was the only child in the family so our food ration book was thin.

My Dad worked as a carpenter building Army or Navy barracks in such places as Camp Breckinridge, Kentucky; Newport News, Virginia; and Wright Patterson Air Force in Dayton. He also had other workers riding with him and he was issued what was called a "C" Gas Ration Book. This enabled him to get the gas and tires he needed for his work at those places.

Each ration stamp in each ration book was numbered and lettered. Those numbers and letters could only be used between specific dates. Therefore you could not buy ahead or behind the specific dates those stamps were to be used. Living and especially eating based on a ration book was an adventure. It required careful measurements and eating a lot of leftovers. That never did seem too hard for me. I grew up during the depression and was used to eating leftovers, and was thankful to get them.

Rationing was a very real and memorable part of WWII. Those on the home front were sacrificing and going without

KEEP THE
HOME FRONT PLEDGE

FOOD
FIGHTS
for freedom

Pay no more than Ceiling
Prices
Pay your points in full

many commodities once thought essential to everyday life. Few complained and everyone believed it was the absolute least they could do considering the sacrifices being made by those on the battle front in faraway lands. When I entered the Army Specialized Training Program July 4, 1944, I began to appreciate even more the sacrifices of those on the home front.

## SCRAP AND JUNK DRIVES ORGANIZED

As the war continued many communities throughout the nation began organizing scrap and salvage drives. Our purpose was to recover and recycle vital materials from American households that were essential in winning the war. Tin, silk and kitchen fats headed the list of vital materials needed to win the war. Rowan County soon formed a salvage collection that set in motion a countywide, sustained drive for the collection of vital waste materials including old silk stockings and women's underwear, tin cans, etc., for the national war effort.

The committee headed by Mrs. W.H. Rice, chairman; Mrs. I.A. Nooe, co-chairman; and R.G. Barker, collection agent, supervised a project for the collection of tin cans by the Rowan County troops of the Boy Scouts of America. They distributed pamphlets which explained the methods of preparing tin cans, listed the kind of tin cans

School children gather after school and search for scrap metal in vacant lot Morehead, Kentucky.

not wanted, and gave complete information on the drive. Collections began the next week after the pamphlet was distributed.

Tin was needed in many phases of our war efforts. It was said that manufacturing one Flying Fortress required from five to seven pounds of pure tin in the aluminum of each plane. It was a necessary ingredient in the bearing of every tank and plane in the armed forces. Tin was used in the face of gas masks and had a pharmaceutical use as a pain deadener and blood purifier. Tin was a must in transporting food to armies overseas. Glass would be too heavy and breakage loss was too great. Our first tin drive collected 9,000 tin cans; and 22 pounds of pure tin was salvaged from those cans. It was vital that the older supply of tin cans be salvaged because the new ones contained 25 percent less tin.

There was also a drive to collect silk hosiery, including silk, nylon, silk and rayon mixed, silk and cotton mixed, nylon and rayon mixed, and nylon and cotton mixed. Silk was used for gun powder bags because it burns completely and leaves no hot ashes. That made it possible to recharge big guns on our battle ships with greater speed than if the barrel had to be cleaned

# Rowan County Still Far Short of Required Scrap in State Wide Scrap Drive

after firing each charge. Nylon was taken to the air in thousands of parachutes, replacing silk in that equipment. Kitchen grease was essential for the war.

## JUNK DRIVES

Those junk drives and scrap metal were a vital part of the home front war effort, because America's home front soon was organized into "America Junk Front." Among the battle cries of WWII on the home front was the slogan, "Let's scrap the Japs and junk the Huns." Ironically, prior to WWII there was a demand for scrap iron and metal. But it was all shipped to Japan. Sadly, many of the guns used to kill our men in WWII, came from American scrap metal.

## AMERICAN JUNK RALLY

Early in 1942, there was an American Junk Rally. All citizens were asked to get their junk ready and call their local junk dealer. He would then come and gather it up. It was pointed out that junk was needed for war, and that in the average American home, basement or garage there was 130 pounds of junk that would probably eventually be destroyed. That was the first recycling in America—which, after 70 years, has finally achieved a new status. People helped the war effort by gathering up junk. Also it was pointed out that every single

# YOU CAN DO IT— EVEN WITH RATIONING

With the rationing of meats and cooking fats and oils, you naturally have less fats. You're using them carefully. Using them over and over again.

But the Government doesn't want your fats—even to make gunpowder—until you've gotten all the food use out of them.

When you have finished cooking with them—when they are too dark or too strong flavored to cook with—then save them for gun-powder. Pan drippings, soup skimmings, old shortening, *any* kind of fats—*save* them—and turn them in promptly to your meat dealer.

Even with rationing, the average family of four persons can buy, on the point system, four-hundred-and-sixteen pounds of meat a year and another one-hundred-and-thirty pounds of butter and shortening. Out of all this, the Government is asking for only twelve pounds of recovered fat, a year.

A tablespoonful a day—that's the least you can contribute to victory. And if you can save more than a tablespoon of fat—this country needs every drop—desparately.

# LET'S SAVE...AND SAVE LIVES!

# JUNK RALLY

### Get Your JUNK Ready And Bring It To

### The Junk Dealer. Or He Will Come For

### IT If You Will Only Call Him.

There's
## 130 Lbs.
of Junk in your
home!

In the attic or cellar of the average home there is 130 lbs. of junk. In ordinary times, it would stay there to gather dust. Or it would be destroyed.

But this is war. America needs every single pound of that junk— every pound of scrap metal, scrap rubber, and old rags. It is needed to make ships and shells, tires for jeeps, bombs, shells, guns.

Gather it up today. And then rush it. Sell it to a junkman. Or give it to a local charity. Remember, your junk can win the war.

Well organized "Junk Rallies" held nationwide.

pound of scrap iron, metal, rubber, and old rags was needed to not only help in the war effort—some extra cash could be made by cleaning out garages, basements, and barns.

I spent many hours during the early days of WWII before I entered the Army helping to gather up scrap iron, paper, aluminum, and tin foil from Lucky Strike cigarettes. That tin foil around those cigarettes was changed to a heavy green paper. But the older packs out in the market were covered with tin foil needed for the war effort. That cigarette company proudly proclaimed, "Lucky Strike Green has gone to war," because those cigarettes were wrapped in green paper instead of tin foil. In the attics and cellars of homes, in garages, tool sheds, and on farms was a lot of junk which was doing no good where it was, but which was needed at once to help smash the Axis armies. Americans at home felt themselves a vital part of the war effort.

Scrap iron and steel came from old radiators, lengths of pipe, refrigerators, garbage pails, and broken garden tools. This rusty, old "scrap" was actually refined steel, with most impurities removed, and could be quickly melted with new metal in the form of pig iron to produce highest quality steel for our war machines.

By 1943, Americans were told that unless at least 6,000,000 additional tons of scrap steel could be located immediately, the maximum rate of war productions could not be maintained and the necessary tanks, guns, and ships could not be produced. The rubber situation was critical too. There was a continued need for large quantities of scrap rubber and other waste materials and metals like brass, copper, zinc, lead, and tin. America answered the challenge by rounding up these materials. The junk collected was bought by industry from scrap dealers at established government-controlled prices to help America win the war.

## VICTORY BOOK DRIVE

With the shortage of paper, few books were published during the war years. In order to provide books for our military personnel, there was a nation-wide "Victory Book Drive" sponsored by the American Library Association. Morehead State College Librarian, Alice Palmer Morris, was the chairperson of Morehead's local Victory Book Drive. It was publically announced that on a specific night anyone with books to donate would leave their porch light on and volunteers would come by and collect the books. People who donated books really felt they were contributing to war effort. All books collected were sent through the American Red Cross to the United Services Organization. From there they were sent to camp libraries throughout the United States, and around the world on ships, submarines, and wherever American Military personnel were stationed. They were also placed in base hospitals and did much to keep up the morale of those in the hospitals. I was in two different hospitals and experienced firsthand the benefit of those books. It sure did help to keep up my morale. I was also a guard at one time at a base hospital in Germany where those books brought a little bit of home to those far from home.

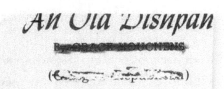

An Old Dishpan

( )

The old battered dish pan
Held the dishes every day;
A job without a "future"
I "nearly" heard it say.

Now that old pan was alumin
So it joined a million more,
To help defend our country,
And guard our peaceful shore.

You wouldn't know it now,
That plain old battered thing,
For it is bright and shiny,
Out on a bomber's wing.

If it could talk, I'm sure
We'd hear a thrilling story,
To rise from lowly dishes,
To fly on wings of glory.

Giving pans is lots of fun;
Let's help all we can,
For when a plane flies over,
"There goes my old dish pan.'

Old dishpans important to war effort.

I entered the Army Air Corps July 4, 1944. Before entering the military, I helped in many scrap drives. We would ride in the back of a big truck throughout the county and stop at farmhouses, barns, and businesses and pick up scrap metal. We would load it in the back of the truck and haul it to the junk dealer. Those who gave their scrap iron, etc. were praised for their contribution to the war effort. After I entered the Army Air Force, I appreciated even more the sacrifice made by the people at home through rationing and doing without many commodities once considered essential before the war.

# HOW TO REGISTER FOR WAR RATION BOOK 2

1. Everyone must have War Ration Book No. 1 before they register for Book No. 2.
2. Every consumer must fill out declaration form stating amount of rationed goods on hand at time of registration. Or any member of the family over 18 years old may sign one declaration for all the family.
3. The age listed on Book No. 1 must be circled in ink or indelible pencil before returning it to the owner. This shows Book No. 2 has been issued.
4. Any person presenting Book No. 1 with age already circled should not be issued Book No. 2.
5. If there is no age on Book No. 1 enter age and circle.
6. Tailoring of Book No. 1 for coffee.
7. Stamps Nos. 28, 27, 26, 25, 24, 23, 22, 21, 20, and 19 must be removed from every book No. 1 whose owner is 13 years old or under that age.
8. All these stamps must be turned into the Board by the Registrar.
9. The number of stamps removed must be entered on declaration form.
10. Should you spoil a Book No. 1 when removing coffee stamps, give a note to the Board to replace.
11. If any coffee stamps are missing from a child's Book whose age is 13 years or under, remove an equal number from adults' cards of that family.

12. Remember you must get 10 coffee stamps for every child whose age is 13 or less.

13. The declaration shows number of stamps to be removed for excess coffee. Disregard fractions.

14. For excess coffee, stamps must be removed from adults' books only.

15. If there should be more excess coffee than there are stamps to remove, then enter the excess amount of coffee on Book No. 1 to the left of the word (Certificate of registrar)......pounds coffee. Also enter amount of declaration and document register

16. Tailoring Book No. 2

17. Remove only the blue eight point stamps.

18. There are six of the blue eight point stamps on each page and are in alphabetical order. Begin with A and remove in order.

19. The number of points to be removed should be removed equally on all cards of that family.

20. The number of stamps removed must equal the number on the declaration.

21. Each Book No. 2 has 24 blue eight point stamps, and if the number of excess cans is greater than this amount, enter on the inside front cover the number of cans......cans. (Excess cans on declaration in circle).

22. Add all eight point stamps for one family and enter the amount on the consumer declaration.

23. Each person who has a Book No. 1 should receive a Book No. 2 properly filled out and tailored.

24. Regardless of what Board Number appears on War Ration Book No. 1, the issuing Board must show their number on Book No. 2.

25. If a person's address has changed, show new address on Book 2.

Locally grown strawberries were sold at the community farmers market. *Photo: Kentucky Department of Archives.*

## CHAPTER 6

# Victory Gardens: Food Front

"I was hungry and you gave me meat." (Matt. 25:35)

May in Kentucky is a time to plant gardens. In early May, 1943, in the middle of a devastating war, many of us in my hometown were busy planting what soon became known as "victory gardens." Those vegetable gardens were a part of our contribution to the war effort. Throughout WWII it was repeatedly emphasized how indispensable those victory gardens were in maintaining our nation's food supply. Americans' backyard gardens contributed significantly to the war effort in keeping the nation fed and fit as well as providing enough to help feed the fighting forces. Since I was not old enough for active service, I did my fair share of hoeing and weeding in our vegetable garden.

Many of my neighbors also did their share of backyard gardening. It even became a community effort when an empty field on the edge of town was turned into a community victory garden for those who did not have space in their own backyard. It was a place where many planted their garden and worked their gardens together and socialized with their neighbors at the same time. They felt they were making a contribution to winning the war as well as promoting a healthy diet. Local college Math Professor, L.A. Fair, always had a productive vegetable garden in the backyard of his home. It helped feed his family and neighbors during the war years and they ate healthy. When the war in Europe ended, it was pointed out that victory gardens should be continued because the war in the Pacific was still raging. Also, even after WWII ended, there would be an even greater need for food because reserve stock had reached a critically low level. At the same time the demand for food was increasing at a constantly accelerated rate.

Food in sufficient quantities was needed to meet the demands of our nation's fighting forces scattered throughout the world as well as for the civilian population at home producing weapons of war. Also, the U.S. was helping our Allies meet their food shortages, and to relieve the distress of millions in liberated countries that had been malnourished for many years.

The American farmer did an excellent job in the production of food throughout the war years; even with the shortage of seed, fertilizer, tires, gasoline, and trucks, as well as other factors beyond their control. With commercial food producers at their max, the victory gardens of WWII took on added importance. That was especially true because of the problem of distributing the food where it was needed in this country. Railroads were over burdened with men, machines and weapons of war.

Under such circumstances victory gardens assumed an added urgency. With meat shortages compelling more and more strict rationing, vegetables had to be consumed more extensively. At the same time householders had to rely more and more on backyard gardens for their vegetables. It was estimated that in the spring of 1944 during the height of WWII, 20,000,000 Americans planted victory gardens, and more were needed.

But the situation was not without its bright side. Even in 1945, with limited dietary knowledge, it was pointed out that while a certain amount of meat might be necessary for a balanced diet (especially for those doing manual labor), vegetables were extremely important in promoting and maintaining good health. Dietitians learned during WWII really for the first time "that vegetables contained many of the important vitamins and minerals which helped supply strong bones; sound teeth; good eyesight; steady nerves; firm muscles; rich red blood; good digestion; physical endurance; a strong constitution capable of withstanding the assaults of disease germs; and many other attributes of good health."

Milk was also important in maintaining good health during WWII. Milk was sometimes called America's number one wartime food; therefore, Kentucky's dairy farmers were a vital part of the food chain during WWII. They sent billions of quarts of milk flowing each year

Kentucky Dairy Farmers important to the war effort.

through channels of processing and distribution to the armed forces, war workers, civilians and our allies throughout the world. Milk's nutritional importance to good health was recognized around the world and Kentucky's dairy farmers were front and center in meeting the military and civilians needs around the world. Kentucky's milk reached England in the form of cheese; Russia as butter; China and Africa as powder and France as evaporated milk. As a member of the Army Air Corps in Europe, I actually came to like the milk made from powder.

In 1942, Kentucky's 575,000 cows produced 998,000,000 quarts of milk, an average of 1,735 quarts of milk per cow. Kentucky's milk was used in all forms as cheese, powdered milk and evaporated milk, and was shipped around the world. Milk played a vital part in the war effort, and Kentucky dairy farmers contributed greatly in that effort.

Well fed cattle important in milk production. *Picture taken Spring Grove Dairy Farm, Bath County: Aubrey Kautz, Owner.*

## SEVEN BASIC FOOD GROUPS ESTABLISHED

During WWII in the war against nutritional deficiencies, both government and diet experts had come up with what would later be known as the "seven basic food groups." It was pointed out that of the seven basic food groups, three consisted almost entirely of vegetables which could be grown in backyard victory gardens.

Whether you lived in the city or the country, it was pointed out, you owed it to yourself, your family and your nation to grow a victory garden. Such a garden would provide personal insurance against scarcity, contributed to better health, provided fresher tastier vegetables for home consumption, save money, help feed the troops around the world and help bring WWII to a victorious end. It was through American victory gardens that many Americans contributed significantly to the war effort. However, it was during WWII that the concept of those seven basic food groups, the "Bible" of diets for half a century, was developed. Victory gardens were born of a war time necessity because of a critical shortage of food and an inadequate distribution system. The government's promotion of these gardens was an attempt to make each American family at least partially self-sufficient. It worked well on a short term basis.

## VICTORY FARM VOLUNTEERS

It was during this time that farming was hailed as one of the nation's most important jobs. "Uncle Sam" had called upon farmers to raise food for our fighting men, our war workers in the factories, and our allies. With the farmers' sons in the military, and his helpers working in defense plants, more food had to be produced by fewer workers. Everyone who could help was called upon to help. My uncle, Davis Ellis, was granted a discharge from the Navy in 1943 to return to his farm and raise food for the fighting forces.

The cry went out to urge young teenage boys and girls to become a "Victory Farm Volunteer." That was the term given to young people working on farms during the summers. Those volunteers were a part of the "U.S. Crop Corps." Half a million boys and girls volunteered for the Crop Corps. Many high schools organized a "VFC" group with the cooperation of their County Agriculture Agent or the Federal Emergency Farm Labor Assistant. Along with backyard gardens and farm crops, the Volunteer Victory Crops helped feed the world during WWII.

As Rowan County moved out of the Great Depression of the 1930s into the war years of the 1940s, this nation was faced with many problems. Chief among those problems was preserving and providing enough food for millions of men and women around the world as well as on the home front. (One needs to remember that there was no such thing as frozen food then.) Many of the lessons learned in preserving and processing food in the war against hunger in the 1930s were applied during the war years of the 1940s.

### FIRST FARMERS MARKET ESTABLISHED

Rowan County was considered an agricultural county in the 1940s and had plenty of food for local use but there was the problem of getting farm products to consumers. In June, 1942, the Morehead Board of Trade established a community market designed to give farmers and truck gardeners a wholesale outlet and to provide the people of Morehead with a source of farm produce in wholesale lots. It was considered an altogether new approach to marketing in Morehead. Up to that time farmers brought their produce into Morehead and knocked on doors to sell their products.

The new Board of Trade market was established on the grounds of Morehead High School on Second Street. At first it was open only on Thursday, but became so popular that it was open on Tuesdays as well.

### COMMUNITY CANNERY ESTABLISHED

By 1943 with rationing of sugar as well as much of the food being produced and preserved on local farms, it became necessary to determine if food stamps were to be surrendered for home canning and the sugar needed for that purpose, for example, "May I give away as many quarts of home canned vegetables as I desire?" Answer: "No, but each person in your family may give away as many as 50 quarts without collecting ration stamps." Those and many other questions were soon to be asked as this community entered into a new phase of food preservation.

Community Cannery in Morehead, Kentucky provided farmers and backyard gardeners a way of preserving food. *Photo: Art Stewart.*

The local cannery kept many of the high school girls busy. Among those in photo: Eva Fouch, Helen Early, Genalee Blair, and Mrs. Sam Litton.

In June, 1943, Rowan County Vocational Home Economics teacher, Virginia Rice, was employed to establish a new commercial grade community cannery in Morehead. Mrs. Rice had a Home Economics degree from the University of Kentucky as well as a great deal of experience in food and nutrition. She was required to attend a two week course in Lexington, where she received special instructions in preparation and processing food. Mrs. Rice was employed by the Rowan County Board of Education to establish a local professional grade cannery. Her salary was paid from funds available from the Rural War Production Training Program, and she soon was successful in establishing a small community cannery.

The Community Cannery opened on July 5, 1943, in what had

Local ladies process tomato juice during war years. *Photo: Lucien Rice.*

been the WPA (Depression Agency) warehouse, and later was used by the School Board as a Vocational Training Building. The cannery was equipped with the latest equipment available including retorts, steam kettles, stoves, blanching vats and hand sealers. All residents were invited to use the cannery; however, it was emphasized that the cannery was not intended to replace home canning, just to supplement it. Families throughout the county were urged to join district groups in receiving help on how to make best use of the cannery.

### ILLEGAL SALE OF FOOD CALLED BLACK MARKETING

With food rationing there were problems of black-marketing food. If you sold food you were required, just as the grocery stores

"Such a *little* thing"...
but that's what makes

# BLACK MARKETS

Think hard.

Can you honestly say you never misused a single small ration stamp?

It's such a little thing to do — carelessly. It seems so unimportant.

Yet it takes only a single innocent offense, repeated by many others just like you, to mount up into a great national menace.

Black Markets can get their start in what seems the most innocent way — through honest, patriotic people like you who wouldn't do one thing to handicap the war effort.

—people who don't even realize they are misusing their rationing books, or violating the rationing rules.

The farmer who kills his own meat — as he is entitled to — and sends his extra red stamps to a relative in town.

The woman who has guests coming for dinner, finds herself short on stamps and begs her grocer to help her out.

The man who returns the garageman's friendly services by handing him a few loose gas coupons.

Multiply one innocent violation by all the innocent, careless violators and we'll be a nation of cheaters — and starvers.

Take only a little that isn't yours ... and, together, you take all!

\* \* \*

—If you want to keep your skirts clean of any Black Market transactions, do these three things:

1. Make no purchase of rationed goods without surrendering the correct amount of ration points.

2. Obtain no rationed goods, to which you are not entitled, on someone else's ration stamps.

Food rationing brought warnings against black marketing.

were, to collect ration stamps at the rate of eight points per quart sold. Those ration stamps had to be turned in to the War Ration Board. (Who said things were simple in the old days?)

Fifteen hundred cans of food were processed by 26 families the first week the Community Cannery was in operation. For 25 cents per hour farmers could hire someone to do the work for them. My wife recalled working during her youth in the heat of the steam kitchen and the hot August temperatures helping people do their canning. Not only fruit and vegetables were processed but chicken was also canned. The only cost to use the cannery was a small charge for electricity. The canning was done in glass jars furnished by the family or sealed in tin cans as in commercial canning. Since there was a cost of three cents per tin can, most chose to furnish their own glass jars which were less expensive and could be used again. Many people donated glass jars to the cannery.

The Community Cannery completed its first season of operation on October 8, 1943. By that time more than 6,000 cans of fruits, vegetables and meats had been processed by more than 200 local families and a small number from nearly counties. There was even one woman from Tulsa, Oklahoma, who canned and transported some of Rowan County's produce to her home. A woman from Cleveland also made use of the cannery while visiting in Morehead that summer.

## WAR ENDS—CANNERY CLOSED

The largest number of cans prepared by one family in one day was 230 cans of corn. The largest total production in one day was 503 cans. Those were remarkable numbers considering there might be as many as 27 families using the cannery at the same time. Although all types of fruits and vegetables were processed, the only meats canned were fried chicken, stewed chicken and chicken soup. Mrs. Virginia Rice and that small community cannery, along with others like it, provided a great service to this nation during those difficult war years.

# Letters from Home

Mothers from everywhere in the US wrote letters to their sons and daughters during the war. Whether they wrote from a small farm in Kentucky or a small town Alabama, whether their child was in the military at home or abroad, mothers shared similar hopes and fears. Four of Jetta Johnson's five sons served in the military during World War II. Her letter is to J.O., who is training to be a medic. Caroline Williams's son Richard is a pilot flying missions over Germany.

Daniels Creek, Kentucky,
Feb 1943

Dear J.O.,

Your dad has just gone to work. It is now 5:30. Juanita and Donald are in bed. Bennett stayed at Paul's last night. I have to go to Millard to register for canned food today. I don't feel like going as I have a toothache; my face has been swollen awful, but is better now. I will work Bennett and Donald in the garden this week as there is no school while they are registering people. My pig is growing fast. I am going to keep it and raise some little ones as it is the best stock there is.

Your daddy is paying $50 on the place at Sutton. Looks like I will never have any more money to spend. I tried to keep him from it, but no use talking to him. Grandpa Johnson is buying a horse to plow with this summer. Said Bennett and Cisco Bay could plow, but Bennett is all the help I have so I can't let him go far. I can't raise everything by myself.

How are you getting along in your school? You must do your best to make good. You have some large pictures made and send me one. I let Myrldean keep the little one till Friday. You must be a good boy and make the best you can of your duty and maybe you won't have to fight. Write me about Utah, what you have seen of it. Dwight sent his picture home. I think you should send me one as you know I want one so bad. I get three gallons of milk each day and get my own eggs now. I've wanted to send you some candy, but you know sugar is rationed, and I can't seem to spare enough for candy.

You must write Myrldean. Evelyn says she doesn't go with anybody. Elkhorn is winning most of the ballgames. Be good.

Love, Mother

Eufala, Alabama,
Oct 1944

Dearest Son,

Well, here goes with the pencil again. My new found fountain pen has gone bad, but I'm sure you had rather hear this way than not at all.

I'm sick—I've got a terrible cold and I'm mad as everything. Here I have gone all fall with everybody having one and now here I get it at last. I'm at the shop all right but I feel like "the dickens."

We had our first letter from you in over two weeks yesterday. It was written on the third, I think. Martha had one written the fourth about ten days ago then yesterday a letter came in written in Sept. Where it has been all this time no one knows. Emory says he is having a hard time getting her mail. One letter was half burned up even, but I suppose they are doing the best they can.

Today was a big day with us. The postman brought us five letters, then came in around 11:00 and brought another one making six in all ranging from 17th, 18th, 19th back to the 12th. The 19th being the last one. It was a lovely one you wrote on your birthday. You are a pretty nice person anyway and I kinda like you.

I'm so glad you like the book I sent you, will try to send you some more. They only cost $.25 and are copies of $2.50 and $3.00 books. I have two pair of woolen socks that Mother bought for you. I will try to get it off this week as I feel you need them. As to the comb you have one in that box I said was just things that would keep you from going to the P.X.

Molly is still single and just as pretty as ever. I understand she wants to get married. What's the matter with her? She has enough beaus. Is she hard to get along with, high tempered or what? Please tell me cause I like her so much and I can't find any fault in her.

Daddy has written you about Buck I know. Well, his mother told me this morning that the government had sent her the D.F.C, air medal and something else, I've forgotten so he must be on his way home…. He will have a lot to tell I'm sure. All his crew escaped their prison and were taken back to their old base in Italy.

Mother is suppose to go to sister (she has been sick), but Mother has taken my cold and I'm afraid she can't get off this week. Write Sister sometimes she'll appreciate it.

Can't think of anymore. I'm praying for your safe return.

Love,
Mother

(*Caroline Williams' letter is drawn from letters on the website that Richard Williams Jr.'s family set up to honor his memory. Jetta Johnson's letter is drawn from letters in E. Pendarvis's* Raft Tide and Railroad.)

# THE BLUEJACKETS

---

As its primary support of the war effort in World War II, this campus hosted the training of more than 4,400 sailors as shipboard electricians between June 1942 and July 1944. The U. S. Navy Training School (Electrical) had 600 trainees at a time, coming directly from basic training. The "bluejackets" lived in Thompson and Mays halls during their four-month tours. The sailors went from MSU to wartime duty stations aboard U.S. warships, many never to return. Thanks to the leadership and patriotism of President William H. Vaughan and Dean Warren C. Lappin, the Navy's presence helped MSU survive the strains of wartime rationing and low enrollments.

MSU Historical Marker No. 4, dedicated March 29, 2001

**CHAPTER 7**

# Morehead Navy: Activity on the Home Front

"The sound of battle was in the land" (Jeremiah 50:22)

In the early spring of 2007 I received a call from the Kentucky Educational Television Station (KET) in Louisville. The caller identified himself as one of the people involved in the Ken Burns documentary, *The War*. He said he had discovered my book, *Patriots & Heroes: Eastern Kentucky Soldiers of WWII*, published by the Jesse Stuart Foundation, and asked me if any of the WWII veterans I had written about were alive, and able to communicate their story on camera. The answer was yes, a few, and he came to Morehead, Kentucky to interview me and several other WWII veterans to record our stories as part of The War documentary called Kentuckians in the War.

His first question to me was, "What were some of the things going on in Morehead during WWII and how did it affect the community?" When I mentioned that Morehead was a Navy training base during WWII, he laughed and said, "The Morehead Navy, you're kidding!" When I assured him I was serious and showed him photos of the Morehead Navy, he quickly scanned the photos. He was so interested in the Morehead Navy that was all he wanted to discuss. Here's the story.

## SHIPS AND SAILORS URGENTLY NEEDED

Following the attack on Pearl Harbor, our nation urgently needed to quickly increase military manpower and industrial strength. More ships had to be built and men had to be trained to operate them. During that era, the Kaiser Shipbuilding Company, and others, began rapidly building seagoing vessels called "Liberty Ships." They were needed to transport men and materials to battlefields around the world. The factories also began rapidly building battleships, aircraft carriers, cruisers, and destroyers. Then military leaders turned to the nation's colleges and universities for help. The urgent need for manpower in the U.S. Navy resulted in a Navy base being established in one of the most unlikely places in the world—the small college town of Morehead, in the hills of Eastern Kentucky.

In the spring of 1942, the enrollment at Morehead State College dropped dramatically. There was talk of closing the college for the duration of the war. It was then President William Vaughn and Dean Warren Lappin visited a northern Michigan College that had just opened a training facility on its campus to train Navy electricians. When the Dean and President returned, they met with Morehead Mayor N.E. Kennard, faculty and staff and decided MSC could do

ICKY) THURSDAY MORNING, APRIL 30, 1942     NUMBER EIGHTEE

# Morehead College Selected
# For Naval Training Center

as well as northern Michigan. They prepared to go to Washington, D.C., to apply for a Navy Training Program.

## TRIP TO WASHINGTON BRINGS NAVY TO MOREHEAD

On a windy March day, President Vaughn, Dean Lappin, Mayor Kennard, and City Councilman Frank Laughlin loaded into a 1939 Chevrolet sedan and headed east on U.S. 60 to Washington, D.C. Gasoline was rationed and rubber was scarce, but they were prepared with four gas ration books and two spare recapped tires. They met with Fred M. Vinson, Chief Justice of the U.S. Supreme Court, and former U.S.

Dr. William Vaughn, MSC President during WWII.

Congressman from Louisa, Kentucky. The Honorable Judge took them to the Pentagon and introduced them to the Secretary of the Navy. The rest is history and Morehead State College became one of 20 such Navy bases during WWII.

On May 4, 1942, the first unit of 10 officers and men that made up the ships company arrived, and soon electric laboratory equipment began arriving. William "Hony" Rice, MSC Buildings Supervisor, and engineer by training, worked with the Navy staff setting up one of two electricity laboratories on campus. One was in the Science Building (now Lappin Hall). The other one was in the basement of

Sailors arrive in Morehead, asking where am I, and what am I doing here?

Thompson Hall (now Grote-Thompson Hall). Classes were taught by MSC professors as well as commissioned and non-commissioned Navy officers.

The first group of sailors in the program began to arrive on June 1, 1942. Many local citizens gathered at the railroad station to greet them. The first 50 sailors arrived dressed in their white Class A uniforms. They were met by their section officer and were ordered to line up beside the train and called to attention. They were ordered to march off in columns of two. But as they marched past the powerful coal-fired steam locomotive, it belched a shower of black smoke and cinders down on the men all dressed in their Class A white uniforms. In spite of this sooty welcome, they were the first class to complete the four months course.

## SOON SAILORS EVERYWHERE

One month later, 100 more sailors arrived for the second of the four months of classes. The next month 150 more arrived for their four-month course in electricity. After that 150 new Navy trainees landed in Morehead each month for the four-month program of studies. Therefore, when the Navy Training School was at full capacity, there were 600 sailors in the program at MSC, with 150 graduating each month. When the men completed their program they were ready to go on board ship and become a productive member of the crew as an electrician mate 3/C. The campus rang with the sounds of "Hep-Two-Three-Four" as the sailors counted cadence and marched throughout the campus and community. They had close order drill with rifles

Hundreds of sailors march down College Boulevard.

on the football field. The training was a condensed program of studies. MSC was on the quarter system, and a semester of work was condensed into four months.

I was sent to West Virginia University, July 4, 1944, into an engineering program of the Army—ASTP. Believe me, that program was as difficult and demanding as the MSC Navy Program. In those programs students had little time for anything but study and drill.

Lt. Commander George Walker, a veteran of thirty-one years of Navy experience, was in charge of the Morehead Base, with offices in Men's (Mays) Hall. The Ships Company of forty men included nine commissioned officers and a compliment of petty officers and specialists that included one education officer, ships service officer, doctor and dentist. Evidently, there were men with some writing and publishing experience, because the first thing they did was start a newspaper.

## THE MOUNTAIN CRUISER

Men arrived at the Morehead Navel Training Base after they completed basic training at the Great Lakes Naval Training Station in Chicago. They came from throughout the United States from many different backgrounds, skills and training. But even before the Morehead Base was dedicated in August, a base newspaper was established. It was a weekly publication called The Mountain Cruiser. (A "cruiser" is one type of Navy ship.)

The Mountain Cruiser's staff included Ensign P.R. Daugherty, managing editor; Yeoman 1st Class J.H. Hook, associate editor; Yeoman 3rd Class W.R. Ellis, reporter; and Seaman H.H. Selfer, sports editor. The Mountain Cruiser was "Published by and for the men of the Naval Training School at M.S.T.C." It contained general news of the war, editorials, sports, and ships company news, along with an educational column that rated each section (class) against other sections. It was designed to motivate and inspire each section to try and attain higher ratings against each other.

## MOREHEAD NAVAL BASE DEDICATED

On August 21, 1942, the formal dedication of the Morehead Training Base was held in the old Jayne Stadium located at the corner of East College Boulevard and U.S. 60 (today the site of the Laughlin Health Building). It was one of the most important days in Rowan County history. It certainly made Rowan Countians feel they were a part of the war effort. Almost everyone in Rowan County, and many other visitors from throughout Eastern Kentucky, attended that dedication ceremony because it was a patriotic activity. However, I was still in high school preparing to enter the Army and did not attend.

The keynote speaker, E.N. Lunquist, Commander of the Great Lakes Naval Training Center in Chicago, emphasized that Morehead would help build Navy men out of American raw material. Others who spoke that day included U.S. Senator (and later Vice-President) Alben Barkley, Governor Keen Johnson, and MSC President William Vaughn. (Local speakers emphasized how thankful they were to be a part of America's war efforts.)

Dormitory space was provided for the "blue jackets" in Thompson Hall and Men's (Mays) Halls. By Christmas 1942, both were filled to capacity with sailors. Their mess hall was the College cafeteria, where they enjoyed much better food than they would later get in any ship's galley. The ship's hospital was located on the third floor of Allie Young Hall. Also, the canteen, laundry, press shop and barber shop were located in the basement of Thompson Hall. (My uncle, Davis Ellis, was a civilian employee in charge of the canteen, barber shop, and laundry in Thompson Hall, and my best friend Meredith Mynhier, a senior at Breckinridge High School, worked part-time at 25 cents per hour in the press shop.)

The blue jacketed sailors (wearing white in summer) marched to their class in the Science Building (Lappin Hall). The College Administration Building was in what is now Rader Hall. The basement of Thompson Hall was also where the electrical laboratory was located. The sailors drilled on the athletic field, exercised in the gymnasium and practiced lifesaving techniques in the swimming pool. They also had regular required study periods in the Johnson Camden Library. They kept a rigid schedule of 40 hours of class work and supervised study per week in addition to all the above activities.

Graduation meant they were fit for sea duty in Uncle Sam's Navy ships or submarines. Navy certificates and ratings were awarded to the men by Lt. Commander George Walker, commanding officer. The first graduating unit at Morehead completed a 16-week course in electrical theory, laboratory procedure, tool instruction, mathematics and naval indoctrination. The next class, scheduled to graduate a month later consisted of almost 150 men. The school then had four divisions and an enrollment of 400 men working toward petty officer ratings intended to make them fit for active sea duty aboard all kinds of naval craft.

The graduation ceremony included short talks by President W.H. Vaughn President of the college and Commander Walker. In addition, an informal farewell party for the sailors was held in the college cafeteria, which was then located in the basement of Allie Young Hall. Many of the top students in each graduating class were sent to advance training that prepared them for submarine warfare, amphibious warfare or mine-sweeping. Those men were selected on the basis of academic studies, conduct, and leadership skills.

Sailors at rest before MSC's Thompson Hall (Now Grote-Thompson).

## MEN UNDERGO ACCELERATED TRAINING

The Morehead Sailors underwent a very intensive course of training in electricity to prepare them to go aboard ships in our fleets and to immediately fit in the ship's organization and to put their training to good use. Because of war conditions, it was necessary to accelerate the training less than two-thirds the time taken during peacetime training. In spite of this, the men were actually getting more technical training than ever before. The men spent long hours of intensive study in order to meet the required standards. The old adage "All work and no play makes Jack a dull boy" was truer then than ever. To keep the men from getting fed up with the training, wholesome recreation away

Sailors pose for a photo in the ship's canteen in Grote-Thompson Hall.

from the military atmosphere of the school was essential. Providing an opportunity for their recreation was a role the civilian population played. The campus base also provided a recreation program for the sailors. There was a movie theater, swimming pool, tennis courts and a baseball field, though the sailors had little time to use those facilities during the week. Caring for the recreational need of the sailors was a cooperative effort between the Navy and the local citizens.

## WEEKEND LIBERTY IN MOREHEAD

Although the sailors remained on campus in some aspect of their training 24/7 all week long, their dorms emptied on the week-end when they were given liberty from 12:00 noon Saturday to midnight Sunday (if they had no demerits). The campus was quiet on Saturday and Sunday, but the community was filled with blue jackets on Saturday night.

When they were given weekend "shore leave," they would usually let off a little steam. Beer and whisky were available since Morehead was "wet" in 1942. Alcohol was sold at liquor stores, restaurants, poolrooms and other establishments throughout the city. However, members of the "Shore Patrol" (Navy's own Police Patrols) were very visible and usually kept the sailors under strict control. One of the favorite places for the Navy trainees to hang out while on liberty was the Greyhound Bus Station and Restaurant located at the corner of Carey Avenue and Main Street. They could get a good meal served with beer accompanied by jukebox music.

Melvin Frank Laughlin, son of the owner of the Greyhound Restaurant shared this account: "I was about 12-years old at the time and my job at the restaurant was to keep plenty of beer in glass bottles on ice. (They did not sell beer on tap.) The beer bottles would get wet in the ice and the labels would slip off easily. The sailors discovered they could stick the labels on their billfolds and throw their billfolds on the ceiling and the labels would usually stick on the ceiling and their billfolds fall down. It got to be a contest with them and they became very proficient." Mel's job on Sunday morning (no beer sold on Sunday) was to scrape the Schlitz, Hudepohl, and Budweiser labels off the ceiling of the bus station.

When the sailors were given liberty on the weekends, there was a lot of activity in town. Many teenagers would hang around outside the USO and local restaurants with their shoeshine boxes. They were kept busy shining shoes for the sailors, who were good tippers. I was not involved in that business, but I did deliver special delivery letters in Morehead during part of that era. The sailors received many special deliveries, but I only had to deliver them to the ship's post office in the basement of Thompson Hall.

Beulah Stewart, local seamstress, ran a sewing shop in what

was Allie Young's old law office. It was adjacent to the campus, and she stayed busy doing alterations and sewing on insignias. The restaurants, poolroom, drug stores, and local businesses looked forward to Saturday afternoons when the Morehead sailors were given liberty. On Sundays, many of those Navy men attended local churches.

Morehead State Teachers College did not field a baseball team during WWII, but the local sailors fielded an outstanding baseball team. They had smart new uniforms and equipment and scheduled local semi-pro teams on the weekends. With outstanding pitching and hitting, they were extremely competitive against such regional teams as the Clearfield Eagles, Mt. Sterling Mustangs, and Lexington Thoroughbreds. Of course, those "civilian" teams were made up of old men and young boys because the best were in the military service. At that time, cheering against the Navy team was almost unpatriotic.

## USO ORGANIZED IN MOREHEAD

During WWII, United Service Organizations were established throughout the world wherever American military personnel were stationed. Morehead quickly made plans to establish a USO to help provide a home away from home for the sailors stationed in Morehead. In 1942, the USO committee of Rowan County held its initial meeting in the faculty dining room of the college cafeteria, located in the basement of Allie Young Hall. Dr. J.D. Falls, county chairman, discussed the purpose and plans of USO. After discussions of the various phases of the campaign drive, it was decided that the next meeting would be held in the courthouse Monday evening, May 18, at 8:00 o'clock. The program at that meeting was to explain the purpose of the USO to all the citizens who wished to attend.

Commander Walker said, "As is usual, when a large number of

service men are assembled, certain undesirable elements appear to prey upon these men. The best way to meet this problem is for the substantial and respectable citizens to provide social activities which will be more attractive to our normal American youths than the dubious pleasure offered by those harpies. It is my great pleasure to assure you that this is being done in a most satisfactory manner. Week after week, reports come to my attention of the good times our men are having each weekend. That these reports are not exaggerated is substantiated by the almost total absence of reports concerning men getting into trouble or mischief while on liberty."

Lt. Commander George Walker was Commander of the Morehead Base.

That meeting opened following a parade led by the college band, under the direction of Professor M.E. George. Next the band assembled on the courthouse lawn for several patriotic numbers. The crowd then moved into the courthouse for the remainder of the program. Mayor N.E. Kennard gave a brief welcoming address and introduced the chairman, J.D. Falls, who presided. The following speakers made four minute addresses: President Wm. H. Vaughn, Mr. C.P. Caudill, Mr. Claude Vencil, Rev. B.H. Kazee, Mrs. Claude Kessler, Rev. A.E. Landolt, John Rose, and Dr. G.C. Banks. Following these speeches, the program was turned over to Commander Walker who expressed his appreciation for a USO in Morehead. He apologized for his lack of cooperation, saying:

We, in the Naval Training School, are still so preoccupied with the problem of organizing the school to meet the Navy's requirements, that we have a tendency to overlook the important role the residents of Eastern Kentucky play in organizing the USO. I wish to take this opportunity on behalf of the officers and especially the men of this school to extend our heartfelt appreciation and thanks to those residents for all they have done and are doing to entertain our men in their leisure hours.

## USO: A HOME AWAY FROM HOME

The problem of providing recreation, entertainment and desirable social activities for such a large number of men in comparatively small town was a serious one, but one which was met by the citizens of Morehead and Rowan County. Other Eastern Kentucky communities including Mt. Sterling, Owingsville, Olive Hill, Flemingsburg, Ashland, and Lexington also took an active part in supporting the USO.

The local USO was organized to provide a place where the sailors could go and get refreshments, food, music, and wholesome entertainment. It was located near the corner of Main Street and College Boulevard in a building donated for that purpose by local business man Parnell Martindale. Other towns would be responsible on certain nights for sponsoring events for the Navy at the Morehead USO. Many times they held drawings and the winner would get a free long distance call home.

One of the logistical problems was finding housing for the families of married Navy personnel. There was an acute shortage of housing, not only in Morehead, but everywhere in the country. One of the functions of the USO was to help find housing for married sailors and their families.

The Morehead Naval Training Program brought this community closer together as we became more a part of the war effort. That was especially true when you would see 600 sailors marching in full dress uniform down College Boulevard with weapons on their shoulders. That got the attention of everyone. You would hear the cadence called loud and clear: Hep-2-3-4 as they marched to classes, to the ship's mess, to physical training, classroom instruction, and swimming. They practiced water lifesaving techniques in the nude at the College swimming pool. Of course, the windows were not transparent, but sometimes they were open a little at the bottom, and there was a well-beaten path through the grass to those windows, supposedly made by the college girls.

### SAILORS REMEMBER MOREHEAD EXPERIENCE

Commander Walker lived across the street from Janis Caudill on East Second Street. A blue jacketed driver picked him up each morning and brought him home each evening. His aide, Lt. Colliendro, and his lovely bride lived across the street from me on Lyons Avenue where a driver also picked him up each morning and brought him home each evening. For years after Janis and I were married we argued over who actually lived across the street from the Navy Commander. She won that argument. I had just always assumed that if the officer who lived across the street from had a driver at his disposal, he must be the commander.

During WWII many Moreheadians opened their homes to visiting families of married sailors. Some of those men did not survive the war, but those who did survive always had fond memories of Morehead. Some even brought their families back to Morehead for

# Armed Forces Radio Service (AFRS)

In addition to the USOs and perhaps of even greater importance for battle-weary soldiers was the Armed Forces Radio Service. Beginning in 1942, World War II, Armed Forces Radio programs were recorded onto 16" 78 RPM shellac records and sent to overseas stations in different parts of the world to broadcast via short-wave radio to US troops stationed abroad. Programming included information and entertainment. The most popular shows in these broadcasts were "Command Performance," "Mail Call," "G.I. Journal," "Jubilee," and G.I. Jive." The AFRS headquarters was in Hollywood, where talent was readily available. Many celebrities appeared on the shows, often in response to requests from GIs themselves. The theme song for "Command Performance" was "Over There," and soldiers fighting "over there" listened from afar to some of their favorite singers and comedians. Dinah Shore made more appearances than any other star on "Command Performance," but Bing Crosby and Bob Hope made almost as many appearances. The "G.I. Journal" show also included popular songs, by such major recording stars as Lena Horne. The shows weren't only done by stars, however. "G.I. Jill" was the stage name for Martha Wilkerson, a young woman who worked with the U.S. Office of War Information. Her upbeat and slightly flirtatious patter and girlish voice made her popular as a disc jockey on the "G.I. Jive" show and on her own show, "Jill's Jukebox." She took requests from servicemen, and played what they wanted to hear. A recording of one of her shows (that can be heard on YouTube) has Jill playing Nat King Cole's "Don't Cry, Crybaby" in response to a request from a hospitalized soldier on Guam. Many of these stars' reputations were made during the war. Betty Grable, whose starring role in the 1943 "Sweet Rosie O'Grady" helped make her pin-up poster the most popular of any others, was happy to perform on radio programs for Armed Forces Radio. The stars' performances helped the war effort, and boosted the stars' popularity. Singing such new hits as "I'll Be Seeing You," "Is You Is or Is You Ain't (My Baby)," Swinging on a Star," and "It Had to be You," as well as older songs, like Hoagy Carmichael's "Stardust," brought box office receipts way up for entertainers like James Cagney, Judy Garland, the Andrews Sisters, Groucho Marx, Jack Benny, and Doris Day.

HEP-2-3-4 rang out loud and clear as the Sailors marched across campus and streets of Morehead.

a visit after the war. Morehead became much more widely known because of the Navy Training School and their contributions to the war effort.

By becoming a Navy base during WWII, the college was able to remain open. Otherwise, it would have closed during the war years. The contract benefited both the college and the military. For allowing the Navy to train on campus, the college received about $600,000 annually from the Department of the Navy to cover instruction, board and dormitory facilities. Morehead State Teachers College granted the Navy use of most of their new science building, one of the largest college buildings in the south. They also granted use of the auditorium, gymnasium, stadium, and natatorium, which housed the excellent indoor swimming pool on campus. Thompson Hall and Men's Hall combined—with double-deck bunks—had a capacity of 600. Later, it was said, quarters for upward of 1,000 men could be housed by using triple deck beds. Some remodeling had been done to meet the Navy's specifications. While this work was being completed, the female students on campus were all moved to Fields Hall, and the male civilian students were assigned to the upper three floors of Allie Young Hall.

The sailors' ship's galley (mess hall) was in the college cafeteria in the basement of Allie Young Hall. Of course all the civilian campus personnel ate in the cafeteria, too; but there was a separate section for all the Navy personnel. The sailors were all under strict military discipline, and there was no fraternizing during the meals between sailors and civilians, male or female—except sometimes when sailors would see a pretty campus coed, one sailor might say, "hubba, hubba," quietly to another.

The college was required to employ twenty new instructors, and the institution continued to offer regular college courses throughout the war years. By the summer of 1944, the Navy's need for electricians began to wane. By then only those with top grades at Morehead were classified as Electricians Mates 3rd Class.

## THE FLEET'S IN

Moreheadians wholeheartedly welcomed the sailors to their community. They were proud of the fact that their city and college was selected among the colleges of this nation to help serve our Navy, and it united them in the war effort. Local residents extended to each sailor from Commander Walker down to the last seaman, a hearty and sincere welcome, and we hoped they would make Morehead their home away from home. Also, local residents hoped the slogan, "The Fleet's In" would be something which everyone could look back on with pride, and a continued feeling that the best traditions of the Navy were not only lived up to but highly developed during their stay in this landlocked community.

I was in Morehead when the sailors arrived, I never liked the Navy. Perhaps one reason I did not care for the Navy was jealousy. There was a shortage of men on the home front, and as soon as I reached the age of 17, I joined the Army Specialized Training Program (July, 1944). But the Navy had already landed in Morehead and sailors were everywhere. There was a tremendous manpower shortage in America during WWII. That was evident with all the men in the country between the ages of 18 and 36 subject to military service unless they were in a vital industry, farming, had many dependents or had physical deferment. But the term "manpower" shortage took on new meaning as the vital statistical data showed during the war years.

## FEWER MARRIAGES, WIDER AGE DIFFERENCES

The shortage of able-bodied men was reflected in the reduction of marriage licenses across this nation, including Rowan County. County Clerk Vernon Alfrey reported there was a one-third reduction of marriage licenses issued in Rowan County during the war years, as compared with the pre-war years. Not only were there fewer marriages during the war years, but there was a much wider age difference between brides and grooms. In the pre-war years of 1940, the average age of a bride and groom was between 13 and 24.

But in 1944 at the height of WWII, the age difference between the age of a bride and groom was much greater. For example, husbands' ages were listed as 46, 38, 52, 71, etc., while the brides' ages were listed as 21, 26, and 28. Brides may have been a little younger, or a little older, since age verification was seldom required. Nevertheless, the pattern is clear; grooms were getting older and the brides were getting younger. Older men were in great demand as potential marriage partners while the younger men were on the war fronts around the world.

That gave new meaning to a popular song at that time by the Andrew Sisters that was entitled, *They're Either Too Young or Too Old.* Some of the lyrics went like this:

> They're either too young or too old.
> They're either too gray or too grassy green.
> What's good is in the Army,
> what's out can never harm you,
> because they're either too young or too old.

However, the marriage market improved in Morehead with the arrival in 1942 of the Naval Electrical Training School on the campus of Morehead State College because over a two-year period, it brought about 4,500 lonely sailors to Morehead.

### SINGLE SAILORS FIND BRIDES IN MOREHEAD

The marriage statistics from that era were about to become "skewed" as single men of marriageable age from all over the nation came to the local Naval Base. Many Morehead marriageable maids soon became brides of those sailors.

### MOREHEAD MAIDS MEET MEN AT USO

Mr. and Mrs. Oscar Patrick lived in the shadow of the Morehead

Naval Base right next door to what is now Lappin Hall (Science Building) on Third Street. They had four lovely and talented daughters. (Also one son, but this is not about him.) The daughters were Janet, Alice, Carol, and Nancy. When the sailors landed in Morehead, father Oscar would not allow his daughters to fraternize with the sailors. But they were allowed to go out and watch them as they marched down the Boulevard to their classes.

However, one day his young teenage daughter, Janet, had a minor accident riding her bicycle on campus, and a couple of sailors brought her home. After that incident, Mr. Patrick changed his mind about the sailors and invited some of them to his home and to church at the First Baptist Church.

It was during that time that Carol, his oldest daughter, met the dashing officer Lt. George C. Hall, a native of Virginia and a graduate of Virginia Tech. He soon won her heart and another Morehead beauty married a sailor stationed in Morehead. They have four children, and Carol is still living in Ohio, but George passed away a few years ago. Carol's sister Alice kept in touch with one of the sailors stationed in Morehead who was later assigned to submarine duty. But he was killed in action.

Davy Carlson was a Navy Electrician 1/C assigned as an instructor at the Morehead Naval Training Base. He came in May 1942 with the first group of staff to arrive, and like many others, was not very happy at being assigned to the Morehead Navy. But during WWII, you went where you were assigned and the Michigan native came to Morehead never realizing he would remain here in this land-locked community for the rest of his life.

Young Davy Carlson from Michigan met a young college co-ed from Salyersville, Kentucky. Her name was Fern Salyers. She was a

Local beauty Carol Patrick became the bride of Lt. George Hall in 1942. They were together until his death 60 years later.

student at MSC living with her older sister Opal and her husband Fred Cassity. (Later during WWII Fred would be sent to the Pacific as an infantry sniper.)

After a brief courtship, the sailor from Michigan married the auburn-haired beauty from Kentucky. They have one daughter, Dr. Rosemary Carlson, presently a professor at Morehead State University. Davy Carslon came to Morehead with the Navy in 1942 and remained here the rest of his life. He was an expert electrician and worked at many of the homes, businesses, and University buildings in Morehead.

### "SCATTEREGGIA" A NAME NEW TO KENTUCKY HILLS

Eugene Carmen Scattereggia from Brooklyn, NY, was a sailor assigned to Morehead in WWII. When he got off the train and saw these hills he thought, how in the world did a boy from Brooklyn get here? But he soon became adjusted and was one of the better known sailors. Also, "Scat" was popular with the local girls. One night at the Morehead USO "Scat" met Chloe Clay, a dark-haired beauty, who was one of my high school classmates. They dated until "Scat" shipped out into the Atlantic aboard the USS Lloyd. They elected not to get married because of the uncertainty of those times.

They wrote to each other regularly until the war ended. "Scat" was then discharged in California, and on his way back to Brooklyn, stopped in Morehead, and he and Chloe were married in Maysville, Kentucky. The couple began married life in Brooklyn. They had

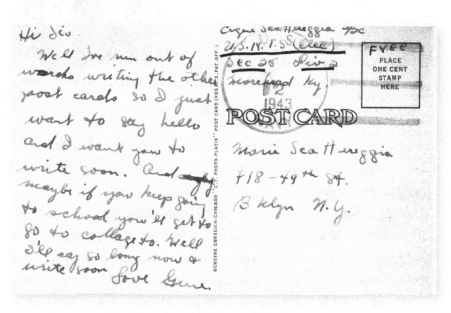

A postcard from Gene Scattereggia to his sister in Brooklyn. "Scat" married a local lovely girl, Chloe Clay. They are buried together in a cemetery in Carter County, Kentucky.

two daughters, one of whom came back to college at Morehead and worked in the Camden-Carroll Library at Morehead State University.

Sadly, Chloe died in her 50s and is buried in her family cemetery in Carter County. Chloe's brother James Clay, a Breck alumni and prominent Lexington attorney, told this writer that years later when "Scat" was approaching death he called him and asked to be buried in the Carter County cemetery. Of course James said yes. Now when he goes to visit their graves in Carter County with names such as Clay, Carter, Johnson, Thompson, and then Scattereggia; he wonders what people think about how that name got there. Now you know how the Morehead Navy during WWII changed many lives for many generations.

## NAVY INFLUENCE CONTINUES

Many of the sailors stationed in Morehead met and married local girls. Some returned to Morehead to live, others took their brides back to their homes throughout the U.S. This is illustrated by something that happened to my wife and me in the 1990s. We were driving through Boston one dark and rainy night, and, hopelessly lost, we stopped at a service station to ask directions. A car stopped behind me and a woman came up to me and said, "I see you're from Morehead." She had seen our license plate. She said she was from Elliott County and had enrolled in MSTC in 1942 where she met and married a sailor from Boston, where she had lived for 50 years. She had never been back to Kentucky, but asked many questions about Morehead and Sandy Hook. After we talked for several minutes, she got back into her car and led us to a hotel in downtown Boston. Also in the year 2002, a woman who had read some of my writing about the Morehead Navy, came to Morehead and called me. She said her dad was stationed in Morehead during WWII. She remembered as a small child coming to Morehead on the train and walking to where he lived on campus and wanted to know just where that would now be located. My wife and I met her at where the railroad depot was once located and took her on a walk down memory lane to Grote-Thompson Hall on the campus of what is now Morehead State University to where her dad lived during WWII. She happily recalled the building where her father lived for sixteen weeks.

Moreheadians have many memories of the Navy, the sailors, and the USO. But there are also many men and their families throughout the world with fond memories of Morehead. Some of the sailors stationed here during WWII, left here, went into combat, and did not return. But many of those who did return carried memories of Morehead throughout the war and throughout their lifetime.

Sailors stand inspection on College Boulevard in front of old Jayne Stadium.

**CHAPTER 8**

# Active Duty — Stateside:
# Military Front

"We have done that which was our duty to do" (Luke 17:10)

## ASTP

December 7, 1941, was one month short of my fifteenth birthday, and I began to count the months and years until I was old enough to enlist. It seemed natural for me to do my part in WWII. At that time you could enlist legally at the age of 17 with your parents' permission. My dad said they would use me for "cannon fodder" and, although my mother would have signed, my dad would not. Shortly after my seventeenth birthday rolled around in January,

**Training Is Offered Men 17 Years Old**

**ASTP Program Is Launched By United States Army**

ASTP, a college training program for seventeen-year-old men, is now the vital concern of the army. Men with educational training are becoming ever fewer as the war wears on. If you are seventeen and a high school graduate or will graduate before March 1, 1945, you should look into the excellent opportunities of this program. It is your duty, for the army needs trained men.

1944, I heard of the Army Specialized Training Program.

The ASTP was a program that allowed 17-year olds to enlist

JULY 6, 1944

# Rowan Youths Assigned To College Training

## Make High Marks In Army-Navy Tests

Three Rowan County youths who made high marks in an Army-Navy test given at the Morehead High School have been assigned to training of a specialized nature at various schools of higher learning.

The youths and their assignments are: Meredith Mynhier, son of Mrs. Clell Bruce, to report to State University, Columbus, O.

Charles Mayhall, son of Dr. C. C. Mayhall and Mrs. Mayhall, assigned to University of Ohio, Athens, O.

Jack Ellis, son of Mr. and Mrs. Lon Ellis, assigned to University of West Virginia, Morgantown, W. Va.

legally. It was designed to train men in such fields as engineering, physics, chemistry, medicine, and dentistry. After we turned 18 we could continue in the program of study in the ASTP and choose our branch of service. Since we were told we could choose our field of study or branch of service and I had some desire to study medicine, as well as serve my country, it seemed an answer to my prayers. The test was given in March, 1944, at Morehead High School to all interested young men in our county who were eligible for the program. There were about twenty from our county who took the exam. The three who passed that test were then seniors in high school, Meredith Mynhier, Charles Mayhall, and Jack Ellis. The next step was for us to pass the physical exam.

In April, 1944, the three who had passed the written exam received a round trip train ticket to Huntington, West Virginia, where we were given a rigorous physical exam. During the exam we were all lined up naked in a large armory. After the doctor examined our private parts, he told us to pee in one of those cups over against the wall. The man in front of me asked loudly, "From here?" After passing the exam we were officially sworn into the Army. Then we

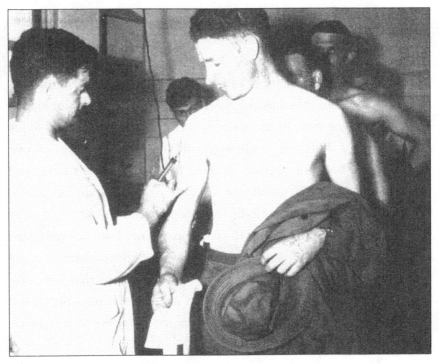

Pre-induction physical exam.

were sent home to finish high school and await orders to report for our duty assignment. Following high school graduation in early May, 1944, I did not know when or where I would have to report, so I went to Dayton, Ohio, and went to work in a defense plant manufacturing parts for the Army 45 caliber pistol. My job was straightening gun barrels on those automatic pistols checking them carefully with calipers and passing them on down the line. Believe me I was conscientious because I thought I might be using one of them sometime. My high school "chum" Meredith Mynhier got a job on an Ashland Oil Company barge hauling oil and coal from Kentucky down the Ohio River to New Orleans. I'm not sure how Charles Mayhall spent that time.

While working in Dayton that summer before being called into service, I was able to go to Cincinnati and see my first major league baseball game, between the Cincinnati Reds and the Brooklyn Dodgers. I recall a 15-year old pitcher by the name of Joe Nuxall was on their roster. But that was only because most all of the major league baseball players were in the military at that time. Stars such as Joe DiMaggio, Ted Williams, and Stan Musial were all in the Army. None were exempt because of baseball even though President Roosevelt urged major league baseball to continue during the war because it was important to the morale of the troops. I can certainly attest to that truth because throughout the war most of my buddies were fans of one of the major league teams and we would spend hours arguing over who was the best team and the best players at that time. We would keep up with our favorite team as much as possible, many times with our ear to a short wave radio and listening to a game on the radio.

## ON MY WAY

My orders arrived June 20, 1944, with a one-way train ticket to Morgantown, West Virginia, which is about 50 miles south of Pittsburgh, Pennsylvania. (Meredith was sent to Ohio State and Charles was sent to Ohio University.) I was ordered to report to the Commanding Officer of the ASTP at Morgantown, West Virginia on July 5. The night before I left, some of my classmates and friends gave me a going away swimming party and wiener roast at the Triplett Dam, which was our old swimming hole. As we sat around the campfire singing popular songs that night we all began singing the recently recorded popular song "I'll Be Home for Christmas." However, I changed the wording of the last two lines from: "I'll be home for Christmas, if only in my dreams" to "I'll be home for Christmas, nineteen forty-seven." I was trying to put a happy mood on a rather somber going away party, but I would look back on those prophetic words many times in the next three years. (Little did I realize on July 4, 1944, that I would not be home for another Christmas until 1947.)

Since my parents were out of town when I boarded the train to Morgantown, John Ellis, my grandfather was the only one there to see me off. I still don't know how he got there, because he had no car and lived 12

Rookie. ASTP, Morgantown, West Virginia.
*Photo: Jack Ellis.*

miles from town. However, I appreciated him being there. As the train pulled out of the station in Morehead at 6:00 p.m. on the night of July 4, I went into the restroom, said a quiet prayer, and looked into the mirror and said to myself, "Well, Jack, this is what you wanted; you are on your way, and you can take anything they can throw at you."

When the train stopped in Ashland, Kentucky, near the West Virginia line, there were about a dozen young boys my age waiting to board the train. Also, there were about a hundred family, friends, and well-wishers at the station to see them off. After saying their tearful good-byes, they boarded the train and sat in the same car I was in. It soon became obvious they were going to Morgantown, West Virginia, where I was headed. I tried to strike up a conversation with them but they were very cliquish and gave me the "cold shoulder," and I drifted

# Soldier-Scholars in the Army Specialized Training Program (ASTP)

The ASTP was the "biggest college education program in the nation's history," according to historian Louis Keefer. It was designed to provide an accelerated college education in engineering, physics, and other subjects of military importance within 18 months, instead of four years. The 200,000 young men in the ASTP program were required to do 59 hours of work each week: 24 hours of coursework and labs; 24 hours of required study; five hours of military instruction; and six hours of physical education. The Army contracted mostly with land-grant universities and with some colleges, who offered facilities and faculty. Besides West Virginia University, only one other college in West Virginia had an ASTP—West Virginia State College, a historically black college that today serves students of different races. Morris K. Holt was one of the ASTP trainees at West Virginia State College. Telling about his experiences in the program, Holt said, "I'd never even been to West Virginia...but I'd always had an image of the towering mountains there. I thought it would be like Switzerland.... We had a great train ride, and on the final leg of our trip from Huntington into Charleston, we all became more and more eager to catch a glimpse of our new home. At the C&O station, we piled on army trucks that took us to Institute. Compared to Texas, things looked so green." Like many ASTP cadets, Morris Holt had been out of school a few years. He said, "Parts of the work were way over my head.... I'd never had physics in high school, and I couldn't handle it. In fact, many of the men hadn't had it, and the teacher told us we really shouldn't have been in the class. I would have flunked out at the end of term one except that I came down with appendicitis and, while in the hospital, I missed finals. I suspect the professors gave me a passing grade out of pity, but I went on to pass the next two terms on my own." (Holt's experiences are described in Louis Keefer's "On the Homefront in WWII: Soldier-Scholars at WV State College," published in *West Virginia History Journal*, in 1994, extends work Keefer did for his 1988 book, *Scholars in Foxholes: The Story of the Army Specialized Training Program in World War II*.)

off to sleep in the crowded coach. Later on I became friends with most of the Ashland group.

## INTENSIVE PROGRAM—LITTLE SPARE TIME

The train arrived in Morgantown about noon the next day and we were met by a First Sergeant who marched us from the depot to the campus. There we were issued uniforms, assigned rooms and roommates, and given our class schedules. I was placed in the pre-engineering classes that included lots of math, physics, and chemistry. (So much for being able to choose my field of study.) That was where I first learned the Army terminology "situation normal— all fouled up" (SNAFU).

My first day there I was given the nickname "Porky," certainly not because I was fat because I weighed only about 130 pounds. But I was given that name because I had a top bunk and one of my bunk mates said with my flat top haircut I looked like a porcupine as I

Physics–Chemistry labs an essential part of the program.

stuck my head over the top bunk. It was a nickname that stuck with me because from then on I was known as "Porky," and was one of two new arrivals that made the base baseball team. When they called for baseball tryouts, I was the first there and went out into the infield during batting practice to field ground balls. After watching me in the infield awhile, team manager "Packy" Golden, a med student in the ASTP, who was evidently taking gross anatomy because he kept a human skeleton hanging in the dugout all of the time, said, "I don't care whether you can hit or not, you are on my baseball team." Although my grades suffered, I really enjoyed the camaraderie of the team that summer and it helped me adjust to military life and

together. Also, Christmas was a time of "hanging out" in town with high school friends and classmates who seemed almost like brothers or sisters. My hometown, the little village of Morehead, was very much a part of me and the thought of being anywhere else at Christmas time brought a chilling sense of loneliness. That was especially true during my time in the military service during WWII.

## CLOSE—BUT NOT QUITE HOME FOR CHRISTMAS

Soon after I left for military service, my parents moved to Ashland, Kentucky, 60 miles east of Morehead on the Ohio River. So, on Christmas Eve 1944, I had arranged to meet Mother and Dad in Ashland, Kentucky, and we were going to drive to Morehead on Christmas Day. (They had been saving their gas ration stamps for this special occasion.) But when I arrived in Ashland, I found my Mother had been rushed to a Lexington Hospital in critical condition. She was sent to Lexington because the doctor who had performed her previous surgery was there. I was to go immediately to Lexington because she was not expected to live. At 4:00 a.m. on Christmas Day, I left Ashland on a train for Lexington which meant I would go through my hometown of Morehead, Kentucky. As I passed through my old hometown about 6:00 a.m., I realized I was home for Christmas. But as I gazed out the train window at the familiar sights, I realized I would not be able to get off the train. Passing through Morehead on Christmas Day, 1944, and not being able to get off the train was like a dream or watching it in a movie. It just didn't seem real to be away so long and now be so close to home and yet not be there. The familiar streets, businesses, schools, and bells were visible through the window of the train, but I could not get off the train. It was then I remembered the popular song, "I'll be home for Christmas if only in my dreams."

When the train arrived in Lexington, Kentucky, 60 miles west of Morehead, I walked from the depot to the old St. Joseph Hospital. There, I found my mother's condition listed as critical. But she knew I was there, squeezed my hand, smiled at me, and that made me feel better. As I left her room and walked down the hallway of the hospital, I was shocked to meet my cousin, Sgt. Harold Ellington, walking toward me. I hadn't seen him for over a year since he had joined the Army Air Corps. He explained to me that his father was in the same hospital for emergency gall-bladder surgery. He had just arrived in Lexington on an emergency leave and had no idea of seeing me. We stayed in a rooming house across the street for several days while our parents were recovering. That night we talked until the wee hours of the morning. He was a radio operator/gunner on a B-25 medium bomber awaiting orders to be shipped somewhere in the Pacific Theater of War.

Had it not been for the somber family situation, we might have been two "wild and crazy guys" from Morehead who spent most of Christmas and New Years in Lexington, Kentucky, 60 miles from our home. Even though I didn't get home that Christmas, it was really good to see Harold and we enjoyed being together. We also enjoyed the attention of being the only men in uniform amid a large

A B-24 Liberator bomber attracts a crowd upon landing.

We marched everywhere we went on campus—in addition to close order drill on Saturdays.

contingent of beautiful nurses. That made missing Christmas in Morehead more palatable.

### RETURN TO DUTY: BUT WHEN?

My mother was still in critical condition in Lexington on January 1 when my Christmas leave ended. But the Red Cross succeeded in getting me two emergency extensions until my mother recovered. Following her recovery, I boarded the train back to West Virginia armed with my furlough papers and a telegram from my Commanding Officer granting me a second extension of my furlough. The telegram said very specifically, "Return upon expiration of emergency." On the way back to duty, I passed through my old hometown of Morehead, but still had to simply see it from the coach seat on the train. During the trip back to Morgantown, the Military Police were very visible on the train and checked my papers. When the MP Sergeant read the telegram that said, "Return

upon expiration of emergency," he said, "Buddy, if I had a telegram like that I would never go back." But I made it back to West Virginia University three days before my eighteenth birthday (January 10), where I found myself one week behind my classmates. That made it extremely difficult to get caught up on my class work. In fact, it seemed I was behind the rest of the year and never did quite catch up with the rest of my class.

The time passed quickly and early in June I elected to transfer into the Army Air Corps rather than continue my engineering studies. I was then ordered to Camp Atterbury, Indiana, for classification. On the way to Camp Atterbury on the train, I passed through my old home town but this time I was given a 10-day leave. But being home in June was not the same as being home for Christmas. Following my furlough, I reported to Camp Atterbury on June 13 and was immediately assigned to Training Squadron Number 1313. Everyone in that squadron just knew no one from Squadron 1313 could ever

Frances Langford, Bob Hope, and Jerry Colona give a show before 10,000 men in a Keesler hangar.

surviveWWII. However, I knew that was just a temporary number and I was not superstitious. In fact, filled with the immortality of youth, I never doubted that I would return. After processing at Camp Atterbury, Indiana, we were shipped out on a troop train to Keesler Field located at Biloxi, Mississippi.

## BASIC TRAINING

There was a part of every veteran's military life, a part many would like to forget, that was designed to change them from civilians to soldiers. That was the cultural change from a peaceful life to learning how to survive in a kill or be killed arena. It was called "basic training" and was several weeks of cultural shock when each man was tested to the limits of his physical, psychological, and emotional endurance. The setting was usually in a hot summer southern climate or a bone chilling cold climate. As future Air Cadets, we were subjected to even more rigorous training than regular basic training designed to "weed out" those who could not stand the pressure.

I lived in a barracks with 50 other men. That group of strangers from all over the country was suddenly like family. We ate together, slept together, and used the same bathroom together. We were awakened at

Pay Day important days in the life of every GI.

Mail Call important days in the life of every GI.

5:00 a.m. by the sound of reveille over the loud speaker system telling us what we would be wearing that day: fatigues for calisthenics or full backpack with rifles, depending on the orders for the day.

Worshipping God in an open air religious service.

In basic training you lined up for everything: chow, mail call, PX, shots, bathroom, church, or movies. It seemed like one continuous line. Also, if you weren't in line on time you were given extra K.P. (kitchen patrol) duty. If you didn't stand reveille in the morning properly dressed and clean shaven, you suffered. Only 18-years old at the time, I was not properly shaved one morning and the first sergeant ordered me to go back into the barracks and get my razor and dry shave standing on the parade ground in the hot Mississippi sun—despite the fact that I didn't need to shave once a week.

There were endless hours of calisthenics in the hot southern sun as well as 18-mile marches with full field pack and rifles. (Being in the Army Air Corps I never could figure that out.) Also, there were hours of close order drill and double time along three miles of sandy

Air Cadets arrive at Keesler Field, Mississippi, 1945.

Every GI's nightmare: rigorous calasthenics.

Gas Mask Drills, a necessary part of every GI's training.

road in the hot sun. Occasionally one of the men collapsed at the side of the road in the sweltering heat. The first sergeant would then run to him and say "Don't waste time, start doing pushups." If you survived, you were a soldier. Of course, there was the gas mask drill when everyone put on their gas masks and entered a low windowless building and mustard gas was released. Everyone was ordered to take off their gas mask just before leaving the building. Everyone came out coughing and gagging, but we learned the unmistakable odor of mustard gas. Also, there was the occasional 3:00 a.m. reveille when everyone was ordered out of bed and the uniform of the day was raincoats and helmet liners. Ask any veteran what happened next. There were the tough "non-coms" and "chicken" drill sergeants who made the recruits' life miserable, but hopefully, better prepared for future survival.

Bayonet Practice, a necessary part of every GI's training.

I arrived as a cadet at Keesler Field, Mississippi, in June, 1945, but the Army did not need more pilots. During the long hot Mississippi summer we were pushed through basic training in preparation for being sent to the Pacific. However, during the summer I developed a serious leg infection and was hospitalized for a couple of weeks and given several shots of the new wonder drug, penicillin. By that time I had fallen behind in my training and my squadron had shipped out. While awaiting re-assignment to another squadron I volunteered to guard POWs. I worked in the stockade in order not to have to stand in the long chow lines. We ate inside the prison and there were no lines. I recall thinking those German POWs had it made.

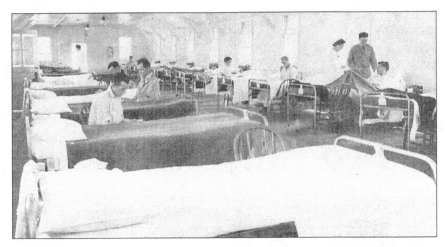

Inside the "modern" base hospital where this writer spent a 10-day treatment with a new "wonder drug" penicillin.

Dispensary available to those on sick call.

## MOVING FROM MISSISSIPPI TO COLORADO—THROUGH KENTUCKY

After being reassigned to a new squadron we awaited our orders which came in early October, 1945. By that time the war with Japan

Chow line long in Army.

had ended and we were being transferred to Lowry Field, Denver, Colorado. We left on a Pullman troop train that brought us from Mississippi via Louisville. I soon discovered that Mert Mynhier, my friend from Morehead, was on the same troop train and we were both being sent to Lowry Field, Colorado. Although we were in different

Barracks assignment at Lowry Field, Colorado.

You better remember your barracks number at Lowry or you might not find it.

squadrons, we saw each other occasionally at Lowry. That trip was my first and only trip in a Pullman coach with sleeping quarters. We were treated royally by the porters and train crew who made us feel important. However as we came through Kentucky I was extremely homesick and would have gladly traded my comfortable Pullman berth in order to hitchhike home to Morehead. But that was not to be. Our troop train headed west across the plains into the cold winter of the "mile high" city of Denver. I thought I was on my way to the Pacific and would probably spend Christmas on an isolated airstrip in the Pacific.

Lowry Field was a huge airbase redeployment center with thousands of men in uniform. As usual, we stood in line for everything. One huge mess hall fed 10,000 men three meals a day. Although there were about 30 lines in that huge building, we still spent a lot of time standing in line.

As the war ended there was no more need for air crew members, and I was reassigned to a clerical school at Lowry Field, Colorado. I hated it. Therefore, as Thanksgiving season rolled around again, I

Propeller
Specialists
at Lowry Field.

began to think about how in the world I could get home for Christmas instead of spending Christmas on a deserted island in the Pacific or in Japan.

## A YEAR OF MY LIFE TO BE HOME FOR CHRISTMAS

By December, the possibility of getting home for Christmas seemed remote to impossible. However, the answer to my prayers came on December 15 when a notice appeared on the squadron bulletin board announcing that anyone re-enlisting for one additional year would get a 10-day furlough and could select their overseas assignment. It seemed like a good deal to me, one year of my life so I

SUMMER KHAKI     OD CLASS A     WINTER OD

STUDENT MECHANIC     FATIGUE

Uniforms seen at Lowry in WWII.

could be home for Christmas. I wasted no time getting to the orderly room. The first sergeant assured me they would speed up the paper work and I could be home for Christmas if I "re-upped." Also, they would get me on a military airplane headed east somewhere near Kentucky. Since my original enlistment was for the duration of the war plus six months, I thought it was a good idea, so I signed up immediately to go to Europe after my Christmas furlough. Maybe I would be home for Christmas.

As usual the paper work hit an army "snafu" and was not completed until December 23. By that time a major blizzard had hit Denver and nothing was flying. Therefore, on December 23, armed with my furlough I went to the Depot to get on a train headed east to St. Louis and Louisville. However, I was quickly told I had to have a reservation. That Christmas with the war ending there were millions of men moving homeward and it would be three days before I could get a train to Louisville. I thought about hitchhiking but decided that was just too uncertain. Then I went to the Greyhound Bus Station where busses were leaving every two hours for St. Louis. Even there you had to have a reservation and they were only taking military men and their dependents. (That appeared my only option.)

## HEADING TOWARD HOME

As I stood in line to get a bus ticket, a young girl who looked to be about my age (18) with an infant came up to me and said she was trying to get to St. Louis to meet her husband who was coming home from Europe. But they were taking only members of the military and their dependents, and she asked me if I would please get her a ticket as my wife. I agreed and she gave me the money. I purchased two tickets. (I suppose the reason she selected me was because I was the most innocent looking.) As we boarded the bus together, we sat in the long rear seat where she could care for the baby.

We left Denver about 6:00 p.m. on the 23 of December in a snow storm, and by the time we reached Kansas, we were in a blizzard with snow, sleet, and freezing roads. The roads were treacherous but we continued at a slow and steady pace until Christmas Eve about dark. As the bus stopped to let someone off, it slipped off the road into a ditch. In spite of everyone out pushing, it just continued to go deeper into the snow. It was now apparent that we were going to spend Christmas Eve on a bus in a ravine on the isolated Kansas prairie in a blizzard.

## CHRISTMAS ON THE KANSAS PRAIRIE

We had passed a small one room country store about a half a mile back down the road so the driver walked back and called for another bus but all the buses were in service. However, they would send a wrecker to us as soon as possible, sometime within the next 12 to 24 hours. The little country store with a wood-burning stove stayed open all night and served hot coffee and snacks, and with about 50 people on the bus, they were kept busy. We spent Christmas Eve on the bus singing Christmas carols with occasional trips to the

Writing "Dear Mom" from the day room at Lowry, Colorado.

little store to get warm, drink hot coffee, and visit the outdoor toilet. (That old GI overcoat was a lifesaver again that night.) Instead of singing "Away in a Manger, no crib for a bed," since we had the baby on the bus, we sang "Away in a blizzard and a bus for a bed, the little baby lay down his sweet head." No one complained, and everyone seemed to be in the spirit of Christmas in spite of our predicament. The wrecker arrived the next morning on Christmas Day about 10:00 a.m. and pulled us out of the snow. We continued slowly along the icy roads toward St. Louis. That's where the girl and baby traveling as my family left me. I made it back to Morehead on December 27, four days after leaving Colorado. That year (1945) was the second consecutive year I missed Christmas in my old home town. But that Christmas would be long remembered as the Christmas I spent on a Greyhound bus in a ravine in a blizzard in a Kansas prairie with a woman and baby posing as my family.

I arrived home in Morehead on December 27 in time to see many of my friends who were in the military service, and had made it home for Christmas. But even though I missed getting home for the second consecutive year, I thought there was always next year. Although I didn't realize it then, it would still be a long time before I would be home for Christmas.

## CHAPTER 9

# Hello ETO: European Operations

"Whence come wars and fightings among you?" (James 4:1)

Following the second consecutive year of missing Christmas in my hometown of Morehead, Kentucky, I reported for duty at Greensboro, North Carolina, in time to celebrate my nineteenth birthday. Evidently, the airbase was full and "there was no room for us in the inn." At 6:00 p.m. that evening about 25 of us were loaded into two 6X6 trucks and several hours later we were deposited at a sparse airbase at Goldsboro, North Carolina.

In about every group of GIs in the military there is usually one that is slower mentally and physically than the other men. He is the one that is usually the butt of many practical jokes. At the barracks, there was one such man whose name was George. One night after returning from being off base on a pass, a few of us returned to the barracks after taps and quietly climbed into our bunks. Unknown to us some of the men had removed a few of the bolts from George's bunk while he was in the latrine. George came out of the latrine and lay down on his cot. It collapsed with a loud noise. Then everyone started laughing in the dark. I sat up not knowing what had happened and then something hit me square in the face knocking me out in the floor. George had picked up one of his size 12 combat boots and thrown it in the direction of the laughter. The boot had hit me full in the face breaking my nose. As I yelled, someone turned the lights on and I was lying in the floor covered with blood. There was blood all over the floor. My buddies insisted on taking me to the base hospital, but I refused, thinking I might be left behind in the hospital as my friends were shipped out. It was later that an Army doctor told me my nose had been broken. It is still crooked today, but otherwise none the worse for wear. If I had known then what I know now, I would have applied for disability when I was later discharged. Many in WWII drew disability pensions the rest of their lives for very minor injuries. Also, many men in the military had received a purple heart for less loss of blood.

### SHIPPING OUT INTO THE GREAT UNKNOWN

Following the usual processing at Goldsboro, North Carolina,

Waving goodbye to New York City; heading across the cold North Atlantic.

that included shots for various diseases, physical and psychological exams, we were issued new uniforms and loaded on a troop train heading for Camp Kilmer, New Jersey. From there we were loaded on another troop train that took us to the dock in New York City. After standing in line for most of that cold January day, about 3,000 of us were loaded onto a troop ship headed east. We knew not where we would land.

The "latrine rumors" ran rampant about where we were headed. But as the Statue of Liberty slowly faded from view behind us, we headed east. Everyone seemed to get a lump in their throat. There was something sad in the heart of every GI who realized he was leaving stateside and heading into the great unknown. On a troop ship crowded with 3,000 men, we crossed the cold, windy Atlantic in ten days. We saw 40-foot waves, whales, and icebergs. Many of the men became seasick and they were usually hanging over the rails vomiting their insides out. I had heard that if you kept your stomach full, you would not get seasick. Therefore, I volunteered for K.P. and ate a lot during the crossing. It must have helped because I did not get seasick.

After our ten-day journey, we landed at LeHavre, France. There were sunken hulls of ships protruding everywhere above the waterline in the harbor. There was also silent evidence of war devastation everywhere, bomb-leveled buildings, railroad tracks, and docks. Our ship tied up at dockside about dusk, and you could stand out on deck and look down on the dock 30 feet below. We would throw candy down to the children who eagerly grabbed each morsel. However, when we debarked the ship the next morning, we had to walk up the gangplank to the dock. It was then I realized just how much difference there was between low tide and high tide. As we marched up the gang plank at low tide, I could see other sunken

# Kilroy, Private Snafu, and Willie & Joe

The most famous cartoon from WWII is the long-nosed Kilroy peeking over a fence. Drawn so simply that anyone could draw it, the original Kilroy graffito may have been scribbled by James J. Kilroy, from Halifax, Massachusetts. This Kilroy was an inspector in a military shipyard. He says he chalked the drawing on bulkheads he inspected to show that he had inspected them. When soldiers saw the drawings on new ships just manufactured and sent into battle, they enjoyed the surprise so much that they began drawing their own Kilroys in surprising places. However, even if Kilroy wrote "Kilroy was here" first, the cartoon drawing of the top half of a long-nosed face, with eyes peering over a fence, had been around for a long time. Some stories claim that a serviceman named Francis J. Kilroy was the original Kilroy. Whatever the source, the drawing with its saying turned up in almost every place U.S. soldiers went. A Kilroy was even drawn, supposedly, on the inside wall of a special toilet set up for Truman, Stalin, and Churchill to use during a high-level meeting. The humor of Kilroy is in his incorrigibility. He turns up in the most unexpected places. He became so closely associated with the soldiers of the war that an engraving of Kilroy adorns the WWII memorial in Washington, D.C. Not nearly as ubiquitous as Kilroy, Private Snafu was conceived by the War Department, with Frank Capra's help, to educate soldiers and warn them about what not to do. In the Warner Brothers cartoons, Private Snafu does everything wrong. In fact, in some of the shorts, his carelessness gets him killed—by a bomb or a booby trap—or sickened by a malaria mosquito. Millions of soldiers were cautioned by this war-time cartoon figure. The most artistically expressive cartoons to come out of the war are Willie and Joe, two GIs drawn by Bill Mauldin.

Mauldin, a GI himself, was called onto the carpet by General Patton. Patton hated Mauldin's cartoon soldiers, who illustrated the ironies and grittiness of live at the front. He told Mauldin that he'd never seen any soldiers look as sloppy as Mauldin portrayed them. Mauldin, who drew the cartoons for *Stars and Stripes*, a military

A familiar sight to every veteran was the "Kilroy was here" sign. He seemed to be everywhere.

newspaper, kept his soldiers as unkempt and cynical as ever. If generals didn't see them that way, he did. And other GIs did too. Mauldin had enlisted in 1940 and was assigned to the 180 infantry. He fought in Italy and in Sicily. He was all too familiar with the GI's life. He was right to draw the soldier's life as he saw it. In 1945, *Up Front*, a book of his cartoons was published, and he was awarded a Pulitzer Prize for his work.

ships protruding above the water and on the hull of one of those sunken ships was a message that said, "Kilroy was here." Kilroy was the mystical comical, smiling face peering down upon GIs all over the world.

### LANDING AT CAMP LUCKY STRIKE

After we were in the harbor, I was thankful the tug that pulled us in knew where those sunken ships were. We marched from the dock several miles to Camp Lucky Strike in LeHavre where we were greeted by a huge sign "Welcome to the ETO." There were several camps at that huge staging area. Each camp was named for a popular brand of American cigarettes such as Chesterfield, Camel, Wings, and Kools. I was in Camp Lucky Strike.

Camp Lucky Strike was a dirty, filthy staging area for the European Theater of Operation. There must have been hundreds of 10-man tents at each camp. Each tent had one coal stove in the center of the tent and 10 cots around it. It was cold! We ate C-rations, but we did get one hot meal a day. As we lined up to dump our leftover scrap food into the garbage cans, there were dozens of young French

Camp Lucky Strike at Le-Havre, France.

boys with tin buckets fighting over who would get our garbage. I'm sure it was the only food they had. They would shout at us saying, "Food for mama, food for sister." However, there was never anyone saying "food for Papa." I suppose they thought we would be more sympathetic to women than men.

At Camp Lucky Strike, I got my first real impression of France. There was very little security. Although the MPs patrolled a rickety fence around the base, it did not deter many GIs from climbing over the fence at night to do business with one of the many French prostitutes who worked the area. It was a very unsavory situation, and I was never more eager to leave a place as I was to leave Camp Lucky Strike in France. I thought to myself, "Any place I am assigned has to be better than this." Little did I realize that my next duty assignment would be like heaven compared to the conditions at Camp Lucky Strike.

## MOVING INTO GERMANY ON A 40 & 8

After two or three days, we were herded on board an old French troop train about 6:00 p.m., into one of those old WW I 40 and 8 coaches. They were old WW I coaches called 40 and 8 because they were built to transport 40 men or 8 horses in each coach. But there were about 50 men in our coach. There was not even enough room to sit on a seat and sleep, let alone lie down. I took one of my GI blankets and made a hammock and tied it up to the ceiling storage racks. At 130 pounds, I could climb into my hammock and sleep fairly well. The heavier guys could never have done that because their hammock would have collapsed. That night we began what turned out to be a perilous four day journey on a slow moving train crawling slowly across the French countryside over hastily repaired tracks and bridges and through bombed out cities. As we passed through Paris at night we were able to get off the train for an hour to walk around and try to communicate with the people. I tried to recall my high school French but soon found that I could not communicate with them at all. Even though I could read and write some in the French language, I could not speak it or understand it. I would later learn to speak and understand German, but I could not read it or write it.

As the train moved slowly into Germany, we saw even more severe devastation of cities and towns. About noon, we passed through Dresden, where we were permitted to get off the train and were served a hot meal in the railroad station. As far as the eye could see in every direction, that city had been leveled to the ground by the relentless bombing. That once proud industrial city that contributed so much to the Nazi war machine had suffered greatly for their efforts in providing war materials and machines for Hitler's aggressions.

Devastation Scene from railway station in Germany.

## BOMBED OUT CITIES BEING REBUILT BY HAND

As we moved through Germany's bombed out cities, it was apparent that the German people were industrious and hard working. In every devastated city you would see men, women, and children cleaning bricks one by one by hand and preparing them to be reused in rebuilding. They were working like ants on those piles of rubble. On more than one occasion, I saw German women harnessed to pull wagons and plows instead of mules or horses as they tried to rebuild their devastated cities. The men were behind pushing the plows or wagons, which seemed to me to be just the opposite of what they should have been doing. As I became more familiar with the German culture then and should have realized that German men were too proud to pull a plow but not too proud to push it.

## GERMANY'S WEST POINT OF THE AIR

We finally arrived at a place called Furstenfeldbruck just outside of Munich. It had been the German "West Point" of the air and was the pride of Germany's Air Force General Herman Goering, because it was the place where the Germans trained their jet pilots. Germany did have jet planes at the end of the war and their pilots lived in the lap of luxury as long as they lived.

While at Furstenfeldbruck I was assigned to guard duty one night from midnight until 8:00 a.m. I had learned that when you were assigned to guard duty you arrived early and got into the truck first, sometimes you would not be needed because you were the last one out of the truck. But that night I had the last assignment. I was guarding a German POW who was in the base hospital. When I came into the prisoner's room at midnight, he seemed to be asleep in one of the hospital beds. I pulled up a chair where I could look out at the snow covered landscape and watch the prisoner at the same time. After sitting there for an hour or more the prisoner aroused up and in broken English said, "Why don't you lay down in that other bed? That's what the other guards do." My first thought was that's a crock of baloney, he wants me to go to sleep, he'll take my weapon and escape. But after another hour of dozing in the chair I quietly crept over to the other bed, lay down and put the loaded 45 pistol across my chest and was determined to see what that POW was going to do. The next thing I knew the nurse was waking me up, smiling, and saying, "Your relief is here." My first thought was that during the American Civil War, a soldier was court martialed and sentenced to be hanged for going to sleep on guard duty. But the boy's mother had pleaded with President Lincoln who commuted the lad's sentence saying that he still wished "They could give him just a little bit of hanging." Maybe I needed just a little bit of hanging for that offense.

Furstenfeldbruck was a magnificently constructed airbase. It was more like a plush hotel than any airbase I had ever seen. The dining room had small tables with tablecloths. There was silverware with china plates and cups. The bathrooms had marble on the floors and in the showers. There was also hot water available. The great assembly hall had individual upholstered chairs, carpeted floors, and magnificent furniture. There were huge oak double doors about 30 feet high that entered the great assembly hall and those doors could be opened and closed with one finger of pressure. The German jet pilots had lived in luxury but now that the war was over it was "To the victor goes the spoils."

## DACHAU: FACTORY FOR MURDER

Shortly before we arrived at Furstenfeldbruck, Germany, General Eisenhower had ordered all American GIs in Europe to go through

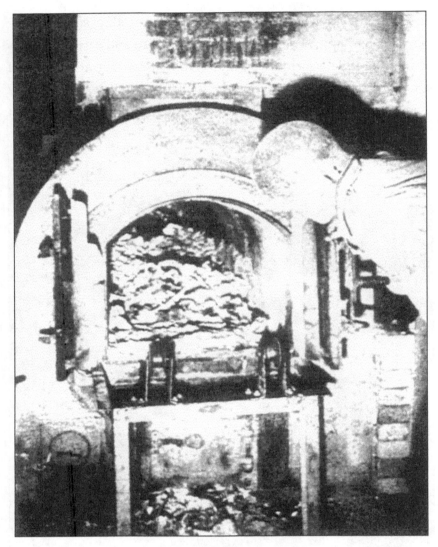

Furnace where bodies of concentration camp victims were cremated

at least one of the infamous concentration camps. His reasoning, according to his orders, was, "Just in case anyone ever denies that those atrocities ever happened you would be able to testify that they did happen." That was in 1946, and at that time I could never imagine anyone ever denying the holocaust. Today, some people deny it ever happened. I went through Dachau and saw the results of those terrible atrocities committed in that concentration camp. I saw the gas chambers where those scheduled to die were told they were to take showers and be deloused. Instead of water coming out

of the showers, there was deadly gas. After the victims had been gassed, their bodies were loaded onto conveyor belts and they were dumped directly into a furnace. However, when Dachau was liberated, the Nazis in the camp did not have time to burn or bury all the bodies. As the American troops were advancing toward the camp, the prisoners were forced to dig mass graves and were then machine gunned and fell into these mass graves. Consequently, today we have many macabre photos of mass graves full of bodies actually taken by GIs who liberated the camp.

There were also torture chambers where people were strung up by their hands and vicious German shepherd dogs were turned loose on them. Doctors performed operations on prisoners without anesthetic. Bodies of prisoners sometimes were skinned and lamp shades and other items made out of human skin. The Nazis kept names of the next of kin of a lot of the prisoners, and when one was killed or died, they would contact the next of kin and tell them to send them ten marks and they would send their ashes. If they

German civilians forced to bury the dead at Dachau.

received the money, they would just send them a shovel full of bones and ashes.

## DACHAU HORROR UNFORGETTABLE

When we went through Dachau, it had been cleaned up somewhat but it was still a terrible testimony to man's inhumanity to man. At Dachau, the Germans kept a record of killing 237,000 human beings, with many experiments on the ways to die and how long it

Ghastly rows of Dachau Concentration Camp victims.

took them to die. Their ultimate solution to the Jews was to destroy them. I talked to several German citizens in the small town outside of Dachau and they said they never knew what was going on at the camp. Perhaps many of them did know, but couldn't or wouldn't do anything about it. Maybe there was nothing they could do given the power of the Nazi government.

After Dachau was liberated, General Patton ordered all citizens in the town to bury the dead, then clean and disinfect the place. But there was still the strong stench of death when I was there.

### SCOPE OF HUMAN CARNAGE REALIZED 25 YEARS LATER

Going through those Nazi concentration camps, GIs like myself—I was only 19-years old—were shocked beyond belief. The horror of the bodies; the factory for killing and destroying bodies; and the unmistakable stench of death left an indelible impression. Sixty plus years later, the memory remains. When I returned home to civilian life, I would tell people about Dachau where a record was kept of killing 237,000 men, women, and children. The scope of such carnage is something Americans comprehended more fully 25 years later, when the Nazi mass murderer Rudolph Eichmann was captured in South America and returned to Germany for trial. All the details of the horrific acts he committed that came out as a result of that trial 25 years after the war ended finally sank into the American psyche. It was only then that Americans seem to realize what happened in those concentration camps. I will never forget Dachau, and I pray that such evil never takes root in America.

T.C.S.—C47s with gliders in tow piloted by Sgt. Pilots.

Downtown Bad Homburg near Frankfurt, Germany.

European conflict in May, 1945, the squadron moved into Eschborne, Germany. Although the war had ended, there were still personnel, materials, equipment, and supplies to be transported by the 32nd T.C.S. Bob Hassinger and I were proud to be a part of that squadron.

After giving us a history of the 32nd T.C.S., our C.O. explained to us that the squadron officers were very unhappy with their housing, especially, since the German prisoners of war, because of security purposes, had the best living quarters on the base. The major told us the squadron officers had recently taken over a small hotel and spa for their living quarters at a place called Bad Homburg about 12 miles from Eschborne. He explained that our orders were to take over the day-to-day operation of these new officer quarters at the Park Hotel in Bad Homburg. Although, officially, Lt. Al James was

Jack Ellis stands in front of Kaiser Wilhelm's bath house that was converted to the Park Hotel, home of the 32nd T.C.S. officers, 1946.

the officer in charge, he would be flying every day and Bob and I were to be the "American presence" at the site involved in the daily operation of their new officers club and living quarters.

Major Reminsnider had been an ace fighter pilot during the war, but after the war ended, transferred into the 32nd and began flying C47 multi-engine aircraft. Even though he had flown single-engine fighter planes during the war, he was very proud of the war-time record of the 32nd T.C.S. and welcomed us into that elite squadron.

Before leaving for our new assignment, we asked Major Reminsnider, "How do we get to Bad Homburg?" He said, "Load up your duffle bag and hitch hike." I said, "Do we need a pass?" He said, "You are American soldiers in uniform and that's all you need. Later you will have a jeep at your disposal." After catching a ride in an Army truck, we arrived at the Park Hotel in Bad Homburg. The Park Hotel had once been Kaiser Wilhelm's private quarters and spa where he came to spend the summers and take mineral baths. Each room had private baths, some with wooden bathtubs. When the German hotel staff found out Bob and I were the new managers, they would almost literally fight over who would open doors for us. The German culture at that time required them to bow to those in authority, and they were continually bowing to us from the waist. That was "heavy stuff" for a couple of PFCs, and we began our new duties with enthusiasm.

The Park Hotel was 12 miles from our airfield in the middle of a small German town where little English

A GI rests in the arms of a German "Goddess" in Bad Hamburg, Germany, 1946.

Jack Chido's C47 returned safely from a D-Day mission.

was spoken. You can imagine my surprise when the next morning as I was getting up I heard a female voice outside my door singing in perfect English the words to "You Are My Sunshine." I immediately went out in the hall to see who was singing and it was a German maid. I asked her where she learned the song and she looked at me with a blank stare and said, "Nix Virstay." She couldn't speak a word of English but knew the words in perfect English to that song. It was then I realized I was at the mercy of a university student who served as our interpreter, and I was even more determined to learn to converse in German.

The staff members of the Park Hotel were all German citizens including maids, cooks, waitresses, maintenance men, artists, barbers, bartenders, and musicians. I recall we auditioned a band

Prayers before Sicily.

with a trumpeter that looked like Harry James. (Yes, we had dinner music each evening.) Also, we had a resident portrait artist. Although some of the staff spoke broken English, the language of the day was German and I was totally lost at first. But after about two months of being completely immersed in German, and understanding very little of what was said, all at once as if a curtain had been rolled back, I could understand the conversations going on around me. I then went around the room repeating what the German staff was saying. It was a special moment in my life and it happened all at once. I soon became fluent enough in German that my commanding officer used me on weekends and evenings as his driver and interpreter.

The Park Hotel in Bad Homburg had previously housed General Eisenhower's personal guards. It was located just across a small park

from General Eisenhower's personal quarters. Both the General and his personal guards had returned to the U.S. and the 32nd Troop Carrier Officers would be living there when they were not flying. Bob and I would also be living there and learning how to manage the place that included a staff of about 50 Germans and 25 Polish guards who maintained security behind our fenced compound. Believe me, we had good security because the Polish guards hated the Germans.

Bad Homburg was a small town of about 3,000 people located in the Taunus Hills (German for Lion Hills) about 12 miles outside of Frankfurt. Before WWII it was known for the health spas where people came to bathe in what was thought to be therapeutic mineral waters. Kaiser Wilhelm, Germany's WWI leader, had a private spa and hotel where he often came to soak in the mineral water. It was there he retired after Germany's defeat in the First World War and spent the rest of his life chopping wood for exercise and bathing in the mineral springs. Our squadron officers made that historic hotel our residence during the spring of 1946.

The rolling Taunus Hills surrounding the town located in the beautiful German countryside reminded me of Morehead, and made me a little homesick for Kentucky's beautiful hills. Although there had been a few buildings bombed during the war and two or three German planes that had crashed nearby, for the most part, it was a peaceful setting far removed from the ravages of war—except on one occasion when the sky was filled with thousands of American paratroopers being dropped in an exercise by the 32nd Troop Carrier Squadron.

# HISTORY OF
# 32ND TROOP SQUADRON

1. **March 9, 1942**, saw the formation of the 32nd Transport Squadron under the command of 2nd Lt. Lillie at Drew Field, Tampa, Florida.
2. **May 14, 1942**, 2nd Lt. Blakeslee assumed command followed by 2nd Lt. Trenkenschuh on June 15, 1942.
3. **June 22, 1942**, the first change of station of the Squadron took place, leaving Drew Field and arriving at Bowman Field, Louisville, Kentucky, June 24, 1942 with movement via rail.
4. **July 6, 1942**, 2nd Lt. Tara assumed command.
5. **July 8, 1942**, the 32nd Transport Squadron assumed its present name, the 32nd Troop Carrier Squadron.
6. **July 10, 1942**, 2nd Lt. Flanigan assumed command.
7. **November 3, 1942**, our second change of station, this time to Sedalina Army Air Field, Warrensburg, Missouri arriving on November 5, 1942 with movement by rail and plane.
8. **November 10, 1942**, Captain Love assumed the role of Squadron Commander.
9. **February 20, 1943**, our third change of station, leaving Sedalia Army Air Field and arriving at Fort Benning, Lawson Field, Georgia on February 22, 1943, with movement by rail and plane.
10. **May 4, 1943** saw the Squadron separating, the ground echelon going via rail to Camp Shanks, New York, for overseas processing and embarking via steamship and debarking at Casablanca, French Morocco, Africa on May 20, 1943 and rejoining the air echelon at Berguent, French Morocco, Africa on May 29, 1943. The flight echelon moved via plane through South America and West Africa until rejoining the ground echelon at Berguent. While on this movement Captain Bomar assumed command as of May 25, 1943.

11. **On June 26, 1943,** the Squadron moved to Kairouan, Tunisia, Africa with movement via plane.
12. **On nights of July 9/10, 1943,** the Squadron participated in the invasion of Sicily dropping Paratroops at Gela. During this invasion Captain Bomar was wounded and sent to the hospital and 1st Lt. Ott assumed command.
13. **July 23, 1943,** Captain Lewelling assumed command.
14. **July 29, 1943,** the air echelon departed for maneuvers at Gabes, Tunisia, Africa.
15. **In September 1943,** the Squadron moved to Castelvetrano, Sicily.
16. **In February 1944,** the Squadron moved to Saltby, England, with the air echelon flying and the ground echelon being transported in ships.
17. **In May 1944,** Captain Halec G. Wilson assumed command.
18. **On June 6 and June 7,** the planes from the Squadron participated in the Invasion of Normandy dropping paratroops on the Cherbough Peninsula.
19. **In September 1944,** the Squadron participated in the Arnhem-Nijmegen Invasion.
20. **In February 1945,** the Squadron moved to Poix, France.
21. **In March 1945,** the Squadron participated in the invasion of the Ruhr, towing Gliders across the Wesel River.
22. **In April 1945,** S.B. Thompson assumed command of the Squadron.
23. **On September 23, 1945,** the Squadron moved to Eschborne Airfield at Frankfurt am Main, Germany and became a part of European Air Transport Service; Major Robert H. Remensnider, Commanding Officer. It was during this time the Squadron officers were housed at the Park Hotel in Bad Homburg and this writer joined the 32nd T.C.S.

*Used with permission from: The 32nd Troop Carrier Squadron, 1942 - 1945, c. 1989, by Donald L. Van Reken, former Pilot, 32nd T.C.S.*

Not a Pass — For Identification only
U. S. FORCES, EUROPEAN THEATER

Hq. 51st Troop Carrier
(Issuing Agency) Group

**Identification Card**

ELLIS, JACK D.
(Name)

Sgt      15360850
(Grade)        (ASN)

*Jack D. Ellis*
(Signature)

Validating Officer *Charles B Pickering*
(Name)

Major      AIR CORPS
(Rank)        (Branch)

Birthdate 10 JAN 1927
Height    5   Ft  8  In
Weight    145
Color Hair    Brown
Color Eyes    Blue
Other Identifying    Scar on
data    face.

ELLIS
JACK D
15360850

Identification
Card No.  C 35718 ✳

## CHAPTER 11

# Occupying Germany: A War Devastated Nation

"They shall beat their swords into plowshares and their spears
into pruning hooks." (Isaiah 2:4)

At the end of the war, during the winter of 1945 - 46, Germany
was still in total chaos and there was little military discipline among
the U.S. soldiers. The cities were in shambles, the black market
was rampant, inflation was out of control, there was no civilian
government, and the people were starving. Almost no goods or
services were available except those provided by the U.S. military.
German currency was worthless and there was almost nothing to
buy even if you had the money.

Cigarettes formed the basis of the economy. The value of almost
everything was based upon a number of cigarettes. (I once gave half
of a carton of cigarettes to a boot maker for a custom-made pair of
leather boots.) Lucky Strikes, Camels, and Kools were the favorite
brands. At that time each GI's cigarette rations were one and one-
half cartons per week at a cost of 50 cents per carton—there was
no tax. They could then be sold in the underground market for 50
dollars per carton. It was no wonder that most GIs had to have a

heavy smoking habit not to sell their cigarette rations on the black market.

That summer the Germans were counterfeiting the occupation currency as fast as it was printed, and they would buy your cigarettes with that currency. One Sunday night all the American military personnel in Germany had to turn in their currency and get a new colored occupation currency. However, on Monday afternoon on the streets of Frankfurt, the Germans were still paying 50 dollars per carton of cigarettes with the new colored currency. I never figured out how they got it so quickly. But no matter how much currency you had, you could only send home the amount of your base pay. Each time we were paid it was recorded in our personal pay book and you had to show that to the military post office in order to get a money order to send home. Before that rule was established, most everyone sold their cigarettes and sent the money home. The Sergeant I replaced at the Park Hotel who had been a part of General

Park Hotel home of the 32nd T.C.S.

Eisenhower's personal guards, told me he had sent home $32,000 in six months. But he was not just dealing in cigarettes, he was deeply involved in the black market.

It is little wonder that when we began operation of the Park Hotel in Bad Homburg, I was repeatedly contacted by those involved in the black market because one of my jobs was to draw daily rations for 100 officers at the base warehouse and to transport them to Bad Homburg. I also drew rations for about 150 displaced persons whom we fed one meal a day out of our kitchen. Too, the 50 German workers at the Park Hotel could eat one meal a day. (Which I'm sure was the only food they had.) Being responsible for that much food, coffee, sugar, and other scarce items made me a prime target for those Germans involved in the underground market. But the guards kept them outside the compound. Another of my jobs was to go to the brewery in Frankfurt and get kegs of beer on tap for our bar, and I had to drive through bombed out roads and bridges to get to the brewery. Although most of the buildings surrounding the brewery had been leveled by American bombing attacks, the brewery had not even been touched by bombs. That was evidence of pinpoint bombing and knowing what to destroy and what was important to save. Also, the I.G. Farben Chemical Factories were not bombed. Those buildings served as the Supreme Allied Headquarters in the occupation of Germany. During that era many of the 32nd pilots flew all over the world and they would always manage to "scrounge" cases of Kentucky bourbon from Kentucky, Scotch whiskey from Scotland, Vodka from Russia, Irish whisky from Ireland and British ale. Those "spirits," along with beer rations, were all kept under lock and key. Since I did not drink, my C.O. gave me the key to the liquor store with orders that under no circumstances was anyone (including him) to get more than their share, which was about two drinks a night and not even that if they were scheduled to fly the next day. There were only a couple of occasions when anyone tried to pressure me into breaking the honor code. One was a captain who tried unsuccessfully to order me to open the liquor closet for him and get him an extra bottle. However, he soon relented and apologized later.

Another of my duties was to look at the food rations I brought back from the base and sit down with the head chef Paul Schrey and work out a printed menu for each meal. Paul had been the chef for the German High Command during their occupation of Paris. Before that he had been a chef in one of Paris' exclusive restaurants. So you can see that this small town boy from Kentucky had no experience or reason to tell him how to do his job. He did it well and we became friends.

After Germany surrendered there were several instances where American soldiers "liberated" property and wealth from the Germans. At the Kronberg Castle near where I was stationed, 8 million dollars worth of diamonds, jewelry, gold, and silver were "liberated" and only one million ever recovered. Also, many GIs "liberated" vehicles, including motorcycles, trucks, Volkswagens, Opels, and even Mercedes limousines. Many of the GIs and officers used them for their own personal transportation. They would take them to military gas dumps and trade their souvenirs or cigarettes to the GIs running the gas "dump" for gasoline. Of course, no one was authorized to have any of those civilian vehicles and as the German government became active, they recovered them. But before that time when many of these men returned to the States, I "inherited" some of that property.

One officer in my squadron was being rotated back home and tossed me the key to one of those long bullet-proof Mercedes-Benz

German staff cars like you see in the movies. For a few weeks I was the proud recipient of a Mercedes-Benz and I would drive into the air field and trade souvenirs or cigarettes to the GIs there for gasoline. I had a great time touring the German countryside with my friends in the staff car until it was confiscated by a "chicken" MP who actually thought I did not have proper authorization for the vehicle. Of course, he probably kept it for his personal use before turning it over to the military government.

Later, a couple of officers who were being rotated stateside gave me the key to their "liberated" motorcycles. One was a beautiful BMW in perfect condition and I continued to have my own wheels after the Mercedes-Benz was gone. However, I loaned the cycle to one of my buddies from the base. He made the mistake of gunning it wide open down a dead end street in the dark. There was a lake at the end of the street and that's where he and the BMW ended up. Fortunately, he

Jack Ellis on his "liberated" German BMW motorcycle.

was not injured but the motorcycle is probably still at the bottom of that lake along with an unexploded bomb that had been dropped there. That served as a distraction that kept us from trying to recover that motorcycle.

I became close friends with a former glider pilot in our squadron who survived the war (not many did), and he was affected with a case of what would be considered today as post-traumatic stress syndrome. Then it was simply called "war nerves" or battle fatigue, and at times he would have terrible tremors and shake all over. I really felt sorry for him as we would spend a lot of time walking in the park and talking. He never talked much about his experiences but it seemed he had missed his drop zone on D-Day and crashed with few survivors. He seemed to feel guilty for surviving, and evidently the "shrinks" (military psychiatrists) had recommended that he have a dog. He was given a large German shepherd dog named "Fritz" who was a veteran of the Army K-9 Corps that had been re-trained for civilian use. When it became time for the officer to rotate back to stateside he was worried about Fritz. I told him I would take good care of him. Fritz and I became pretty close while I remained in Bad Homburg.

Anytime I walked the streets of the town at night, I always felt like I was a target for some former soldier with a sniper rifle. Perhaps it was just paranoia but I would never just walk straight down a street, but would walk in erratic zig zag steps at an uneven gait. I thought if I was to be a target I was not going to be an easy one, because occasionally an America GI would be found dead in the streets of Germany during those chaotic months. Needless to say, I felt much safer walking the streets of that small town with Fritz. However, as our squadron made plans to move to another base I took Fritz back to the K-9 Corps and was assured he would be well cared for in his retirement.

When I was not on duty on Sunday mornings during my military service, I usually attended church on the base where I was stationed. But while I was assigned to the Park Hotel in Bad Homburg I could not take the time off from my duties to drive into the base on the other side of Frankfurt. So, on many Sunday mornings, I would dress in my class A uniform and attend a Lutheran Church in downtown Bad Homburg. The building had been untouched by the bombing, and even though I understood little of what was being said, I could recognize the tunes of some of the old hymns of the church. I would then sing the words in English as the congregation sang them in German. I would follow the lead of the congregation and stand when they stood, bow when they bowed and sit when they sat. Although I was never "really" welcomed by anyone, God knew I was there and I knew I was there, and I always felt better by attending.

On one occasion a famous German Vaudeville troop came to a theater in Bad Homburg for a show. Some of the Germans working at the Park Hotel urged me to attend. They didn't want to be seen as too friendly with me, but I decided to go, along with my K-9 dog Fritz. We sat in the rear and enjoyed the show. It was a slapstick show with clowns, stand up comedians, acrobats, and pie-in-your-face comics. I didn't think it very funny but the crowd was literally rolling in the aisle with laughter. Fritz, my German shepherd, was very quiet during the show until they had a dog show. He wanted to get into the act and I had to leave with him.

Major Remensnider, my commanding officer, was 23-years old and a major. I was 19-years old and a corporal, but we got along well. He had been an ace fighter pilot and had shot down five German aircraft during the war. That's how he advanced in rank so rapidly. After the war ended there was no more demand for fighter pilots. Since he still wanted to fly, he transferred into the 32nd Troop Carrier

Squadron. Like many in the squadron, he soon made the transition from single engine planes to multi-engine planes.

When my C.O. ordered me to assume the responsibility for managing the Park Hotel, he said "You must actually live there, and you won't have to come on the base for inspections, guard duty or other duty." However, on one occasion he called me and said "On Saturday General Le May (the Supreme Commander in Europe who replaced General Eisenhower) is coming to inspect the troops and you will have to come in to the base for that inspection because I can't get you out of it." He also said emphatically, "If anyone asks you what is your job, you tell them 'maintenance engineer,' and you are now a corporal."

On Saturday I was at the field in full dress uniform along with the entire base personnel standing at attention as the band played *Hail to the Chief*. Sure enough as the General came down the line inspecting the troops, he would stop randomly and ask a soldier his name, rank, where he was from and his job. He stopped right in front of me and asked me those questions. Of course my reply was "Jack Ellis, Morehead, Kentucky, Corporal and Maintenance Engineer, sir." He asked me how I liked what I was doing, and I said, "I like it just fine sir!" (I almost added what's not to like?) But my C.O. was behind the general smiling slightly as I answered those questions. I never told anyone this but I had about decided that as long as I was assigned that duty, I would remain in the Army. However, as usual in the military, the situation soon changed.

Major Remensnider issued me an Army .45 caliber pistol with holster, belt, and ammunition. That weapon was usually issued only to officers. On weekends when he was not flying, we would often drive out into the hills for some target practice. As I became fairly fluent in German, my C.O. would often use me as his interpreter.

He knocked at my door one Saturday afternoon and came in with a .45 caliber pistol strapped on him. He said, "Get your weapon and jeep, I want you to drive me somewhere." As we drove out of Bad Homburg, he explained. "We are closing the Eschborne Air Field and moving to a new air base," which meant and we would be leaving the Park Hotel for new quarters.

We drove carefully along bombed out streets, bridges, and roads as we moved through Frankfurt. After passing through the bomb-riddled buildings of the city, we drove to a deserted airstrip outside Frankfurt. This would be our new base. The name of the base was Rhine-Main. Today it is one of the busiest airports in Europe, but in 1946, the only thing there at that time was one building, one lonely airstrip, and a lot of wide open space. We then drove into the small residential community of Buschlag that contained about 50 beautiful brick homes. Many of those homes were two or three stories tall with full basements and beautifully manicured lawns.

Buschlag was located in the small town of Zepplinheim. It had

These fenced in homes at Buschlag became new home of the 32nd T.C.S. officers.

been the home of the German engineers and aircraft personnel who built the pre-war Zepplins that flew the Atlantic. That was where the Hindenburg took off from on its ill-fated flight to New Jersey where it burned. Buschlag had been a first class neighborhood. But now it had a ten foot fence surrounding those homes with one gate staffed with MPs 24/7 that maintain security at the compound. As we drove through the gate and down the deserted streets my C.O. explained to me that the Germans that lived there had been ordered to leave their homes, furniture, and take only their personal belongings because those homes were going to be the residences of

This was the home of the last family to be displaced at Buschlag.

the 32nd T.C.S. officers. They were, of course, paid rent but there was nothing available to buy or rent. Most German cities were in rubble and, at that time, there was an average of one room for every four people. While we were driving inside the fenced-in compound, my C.O. explained to me that the fence went through the middle of one building and there was one family that had not evacuated. As we entered the building he said I want you to tell them they have been paid and the property should have been vacated a week earlier, and they must be out in three days.

We pounded on the door and entered. The apartment was a one-room efficiency. There was a mattress on the floor with a woman and newborn baby. The husband was a very arrogant belligerent former German soldier and when I told him he had to be out of the house in three days and he became extremely agitated. He argued that his apartment was not even inside the compound. It was then we pulled our weapons. He calmed down and said "I fought the Russians for four years and we never did anything like this to the Russians." I said, "Yes all you did was kill them and take their property or send them to a concentration camp like Dachau." Reminding him of what the Germans did at Dachau, made me feel better about what I was doing. I also told him that it was because of what Germany did in Russia that he had to move today. He argued that his room was outside the compound but it was not. He said he had no place to go. I said, "If you hadn't started this war you would not be in this situation today." He and his family left the next day. I was not proud of my actions, but I remembered Dachau and that eased my conscious a little.

I suppose that it was because of my limited knowledge of the German language (or maybe my C.O. didn't think I had enough to do) that I was assigned several special duties. On one occasion I was ordered to accompany a "meat wagon" (Army ambulance) with a driver and a GI patient being transferred to the large American hospital in Wiesbaden. With darkness rapidly approaching we soon became hopelessly lost. However, with my broken German I was able to ask directions to the "Americanish Kranken House" (American sick house); and we delivered our patient in good condition. Then I climbed into the back of the ambulance and slept all the way back to the base.

## SUMMER IN BAD HOMBURG, GERMANY

About daybreak one morning while I was still living at the Park Hotel in Bad Homburg, the MPs came bursting into my room, searched it and found my Army .45 pistol. Immediately they grabbed me and took me into the base for questioning. It seemed a German civilian had been killed the night before with an Army .45 bullet. I was their prime suspect because, technically, I was not supposed to have that weapon since it was issued only to officers.

I explained to them that my C.O. had issued it to me and we needed it occasionally for protection while we were out in the countryside. They didn't believe me and when we got on the base, they finally agreed to take me to the 32nd Troop Carrier Squadron Headquarters to ask my C.O. about my story. He verified it of course and said he had authorized me to have the weapon and they released me. That was not the only time Major Remensnider got me out of a difficult situation.

The fact that I controlled the liquor cabinet at the Park Hotel caused me some problems. On one occasion the major in charge of the base military police unsuccessfully pressured me to give him an extra bottle for his own private party. A few days after I refused his request, I received a call from Army European Personnel Headquarters Section in Frankfurt saying I had been transferred into the MPs. Immediately I went into the base to my C.O.'s office and told him I had been transferred into the MPs. He was a little upset that I had been transferred without his approval. He immediately called Personnel Headquarters and told them he needed to keep Ellis and he would send them another man. I was always grateful I did not have to go into the military police, especially since that C.O. was one that I refused to give an extra bottle of whiskey.

Interior of C-47 with "bucket" seats.

C-47s prepare to take off from Eschborne, Germany, 1946.

Later on the colonel in charge of all European Air Force personnel asked me if I would like to be transferred into his headquarters section in the IG Farben Building in Frankfurt. He assured me I would be promoted to sergeant immediately, and could be promoted to Tech. sergeant within three months. But I told him I was very happy with what I was doing and would prefer not to be transferred. Although he had the authority to transfer me without my approval, (or my Commanding Officer's) he did not, and I always respected him for that. I had made up my mind that as long as I was assigned to that duty in Bad Homburg, I would remain in the Army Air Corps. In fact I was so satisfied with my job that on one occasion I turned down a three day pass on an outgoing C-47 plane to Paris. I had come through Paris on my way into Germany and had no desire to go there again.

One of our officers, whose first name was Benny, was a former fighter pilot who had flown the hot P-47 Thunderbolt during the war. It was one of the "hottest" planes in the Air Corps arsenal, and he wanted to take me up "piggy back" in a P-47. I thought that would be a great experience and said yes. But later Lt. James, a more mature officer, told me Benny would take me up and really "wring me out" with all kinds of aerial combat maneuvers. He succeeded in talking me out of taking that

Jack Ellis and Bob Hassinger hated the thought of leaving the Park Hotel.

flight with Benny. Later on Lt. James and Benny flew Bob Hassinger and me in separate light planes on a flight to southern Germany. I was with Lt. James and Bob was with Benny. We were in light single engine planes and were flying to the old German university city of Heidelberg. Lt. James and I arrived at the Heidelberg airstrip first and we waited for Benny for about an hour. Just as we were about to launch a search for a missing plane, Benny and Bob appeared on the horizon and came in for a "hot" landing. After landing Benny said he had seen a group of German girls working in a field and they landed in the hay field to talk to them. So maybe it was a good thing I did not fly with Benny in the P-47.

On one occasion, my orders were to drive a staff car with a captain and a German civilian from Frankfurt to Nuremberg. I knew that Nuremberg was where the German war criminals were then being held but really had no idea what I was getting into until later. I drove over the Autobahn highway and through several demolished cities, and finally arrived in Nuremberg. The captain who was with me said we were taking a witness to testify at one of the war criminal trials. He did not say which trial. We arrived in Nuremberg where the trials were being conducted in a courthouse near a huge stone jail. Both were surrounded by tight MP security and by a high fence with barbed wire on top. When we arrived there, sirens were blaring and military police were rushing around everywhere. When one MP stopped us to check our orders, he said German General Herman Goering had just committed suicide. However, it was only after I delivered my passengers to the courthouse and returned to the base did I realize the full significance of the event. I always wondered if the witness I delivered to Nuremburg was to be used in the Goering Trial.

While at Bad Homburg, my mother wrote and informed me that Meredith Mynhier, my hometown friend from Morehead, was stationed at Wiesbaden, Germany, about 40 miles from where I was located. One weekend I managed to get a weekend pass to visit him. By that time all of my "liberated" vehicles had been taken from me, so I decided to ride the German civilian bus to Wiesbaden. Mert and I entered the Army together and were stationed in both Mississippi and Colorado together. I was glad to hear we were so close together in Germany (yet so far.) The 40 mile bus ride across the Taunus (Lion) hills along a winding two lane gravel road took about half a day. Not only was the bus crowded with people, it made several stops picking up farm produce including chickens, potatoes, fruit,

Two Army nurses at Wiesbaden Opera House.

and vegetables which were piled high on top of the bus. I'm sure the people in Wiesbaden where glad to see that farm produce because food was extremely scarce during that time. While in Wiesbaden, Mert showed me the local landscape and we attended a high class opera at their famous Opera House. That's where I first heard and

*241*

understood what it meant to say "It's not over until the fat lady sings." When you're far from home, it's good to see a friend from home. Mert remained in the Army and retired in 1980 as a "Bird Colonel." Following his military career, he founded an extremely successful logistic company called "LOGTEC.COM" based in Dayton, Ohio.

While in Bad Homburg, I developed a severe toothache and went into the base to see the Army dentist about getting my tooth pulled. He said the tooth was probably infected and gave me some sulfa pills and told me to come back in a week. I went back to my station and the tooth was really painful. There was a German dentist down the street and I went into his office/home and pointed to my jaw and said in my broken German, "I have a bad toothache and I want you to pull it." He was about 75-years old, very frail, and he spoke no English. Therefore, we communicated as best as we could in my limited German. He said he would not pull it because it was infected. I insisted and since I was the one with the side arm, he finally said he would, but he did not have enough Novocain to kill the pain. But I said, "That's OK. Just pull it." He finally agreed. So with very little Novocain he said don't cry out as the vibration might cause the tooth to break off. It was a painful ordeal but he slowly extracted the tooth which had an abscess at its root. In my youthful ignorance I didn't realize it then, but I could have died. After going to my room I thought I **was** going to die for about an hour. But then the pain stopped and I had no more tooth trouble.

On one other occasion when I developed a severe sore throat, I did not even go into the base to see our Army doctor. There was a Dr. Neumueller who had his office at his home in Zepplinheim where we moved to after leaving Bad Homburg. I went in to see him pointing to my sore throat. He gave me some sulfa pills and said if you aren't better come back in three days. I paid him six American cigarettes for the visit. Later on I helped him out with some food.

Dr. Neumueller seemed to be a very caring and competent physician and we eventually spent a lot of time talking. When I asked him if he was related to the Pastor Martin Neumueller who lived in Berlin, he was amazed that I had ever heard of him. He didn't know that as a Louisville *Courier-Journal* paperboy during the early years of the war, I had read of Pastor Neumueller's plight. He informed me that he was Pastor Martin Neumueller's son. We talked a great deal about his father who was a leader of the Lutheran Church in Berlin who had preached against Hitler's Nazi regime. As a result of his outspoken sermons against the war, he was put in prison for four years. He survived until he was liberated by the Allies. But as a result of Pastor Neumueller's open criticism of Hitler's policies, about 3,000 Lutheran pastors were drafted into the German Army and sent to the Russian front. Less than 300 of them survived the war. Dr. Neumueller said that even though his father survived the prison camp, his grief for those pastors was almost more than he could bear.

There was a German Orthopedic Hospital almost next door to our quarters in Bad Homburg. In the spring and summer months, we often would see those patients, all former German soldiers, out in the park enjoying the sunshine and green grass. Many of them were without arms or legs and terribly disfigured. It was there I saw for the first time anyone with an artificial arm and claw-like hand that could pick up a glass of water. Since it was only a few months after the war ended, they were angry and bitter toward American soldiers in uniform.

During the summer weekends in Bad Homburg, there was usually a live concert with dancing in an open-air gazebo-like amphitheater in the park. German beer flowed freely and you could bring your own beer (BYOB). Even though the fraternization ban had been lifted, the German frauleins would have little to do with American soldiers. But occasionally a few of us would attend those concerts and the guys would drink their beer. (I traded my beer ration for their chocolate milk rations.) But we would keep our drinks all together in a cooler that we carried to those concerts. The other guys drank their beer and I drank my chocolate milk. It was there I learned it's never good to be the only sober one with a bunch of drunks.

Many times some of our buddies from the base would come and visit us for the weekend and we would all go to the outdoor concert and listen to the music. However, one of those concerts almost ended in a disaster. We were four American soldiers at that concert on Saturday night in the presence of about 200 Germans. Many were wounded and disfigured ex-German soldiers. After a few hours of drinking beer, the other three men with me that night were getting high. Sgt. Mike Mulligan, one of the 101st Airborne troops visiting us that night, got drunk and, literally, began to cry in his beer. He said he was going to kill one of the Germans in retribution for his best friend, who had been killed in what became known as the "Malmedy massacre," where German soldiers machine-gunned their captured American prisoners. One of those American soldiers just happened to be a friend of Mulligan's and it was fresh in his mind because that very same weekend an announcement had been made that the American war crimes tribunal meeting at Neurenberg had convicted 70 members of the Nazi S.S. of participating in the Malmedy Massacre. The court ordered 43 S.S. troops executed, including Colonel Joachirn Pieper, their Commanding Officer. Pieper and his men slaughtered 750 innocent American prisoners of war and 150 Belgium civilians during the desperate German counter-offensive in the Ardennes in December, 1944, during the Battle of the Bulge. The brutal S.S. troops were under order to "act without pity." Most of those killed were murdered near the Belgian town of Malmedy. It was one of the worst atrocities committed by the Germans against the Americans during WWII.

It was little wonder, then, that when St. Mulligan was upset. After he got a few more beers under his belt, he began to curse the Germans for killing his best friend and was determined to avenge his death by killing a German that night. The conversation grew louder and he became more agitated and the Germans could understand very well what he was saying. So he turned to Bob Hassinger who was also pretty drunk and said, "You turn and point to the first German you see and I'm going to kill him." All the time I was trying to calm him down and saying, "Let's get out of here." It was evident the Germans were getting angry at our conversation because they were talking in small groups as if they were getting ready to attack or defend themselves. At Mike Mulligan's insistence, Bob closed his eyes, turned and pointed to the first couple who danced by and Mike jumped up in a flash and with a loud "Geronimo" scream, pulled a 12-inch knife from his boot and tore the couple apart. He grabbed the man and threw him to the floor and was ready to ram the knife into his heart. But instead, he pulled the knife back when he saw it was a teenage boy and said, "No, this is just a kid and I can't kill a kid. Pick one of those ex-German soldiers that is wearing part of his German Army uniform."

By that time the men in the crowd were really mad and becoming more belligerent and they began moving toward us with knives, clubs, and chairs and murder on their mind. The three drunks sobered up quickly and all four of us jumped over the rail around the dance pavilion and dashed out into the darkness as the angry crowd of German men chasing us armed with torches, clubs and knives. We were able to outrun them and hide in the darkness until we ran into an eight-foot fence with barbed wire around the top.

In the dark we crawled down under some shrubbery trapped

against the fence with no way out. As the angry mob moved up and down the fence line beating the bushes looking for us, I heard a whisper across the fence, "Zheck" (Jack). It was Danny, one of our Polish guards, outside the fence calling my name. He had been at the dance and saw what happened. He whispered for us to follow him down the fence line saying there is a hole in the fence we could crawl under. We followed as he led us through the darkness along the fence line where we were able to escape being mobbed by a crowd of angry Germans, mostly ex-soldiers. Although we brought it on ourselves, it could have been the end for us had it not been for Danny. I think he saved us from being additional American casualties of the "Malmedy Massacre." Years later while at a conference in New York City, I was telling a group of this experience. One of the group was a TV scriptwriter. He asked me if he could write a TV script of this account. I said yes. A few years later he saw me again and said he had written the script. It had been shown in the old "I Spy" TV show. But I did not see the show.

Danny, the Polish Guard whose last name I don't remember, was young, about my age; we had already become close friends. After that escape we became even closer. He had survived the Nazi occupation of Poland but was brought back to Germany and forced to work in a factory. He had really had a terrible life but was able to survive because he spoke German, Polish, and English. In addition to saving my life he was a great help to me as I struggled to speak German. We would often get on my BMW motorcycle and ride out through the green Taunus Hills outside Bad Homburg. Those hills served to remind me of my Kentucky hills. It was my Polish friend Danny's dream to someday come to America. I believe because of his language skills he somehow made his dream come true—but I never heard from him again after I left Germany.

## CHAPTER 12

# Over and Out:
# Still Not Home for Christmas

"He maketh wars to cease unto the end of the earth." (Psalm 46:9)

It was the autumn of 1946. The war was over and Germany, a conquered nation, was divided into three sectors: British, American, and Russian sectors. Berlin was a divided city, at the mercy of the Russians. As a result, the famous Berlin wall was later built and the Berlin Airlift was initiated to supply the city of Berlin. Before the wall was ever conceived, the 32nd T.C. Squadron was very much involved in the early days of the first airlift. There were flights continuously going in and out of Berlin. At one time the Russians threatened to shoot down our planes going in but later relented. Germany was a nation on her knees and suffered greatly because of Adolph Hitler's attempt to conquer the world.

On Halloween night 1946, I won $1,500 in an all night poker game. The next day I sent home 12 one-hundred dollar money orders. (The ban had been lifted that only allowed you to send home your base pay.) My mother was "flabbergasted" at getting so much money and she deposited it into a savings account for me. But it's a good thing

I sent the money home because I later lost most of the remaining $300 in another poker game—not before I had taken a short trip to Switzerland and bought a beautiful Swiss watch. It was called a Rolex Oyster Perpetual and was self-winding by the movement of your arms. (Battery watches had not yet been invented.) I had never heard of a Rolex but I did pay $40 for it, which I thought was very expensive.

## FLYING HOME FOR CHRISTMAS?

During the first week of November 1946 I began thinking about getting home for Christmas. That very week our First Sergeant called me and said, "Ellis, bring all your personal belongings into the base. Our squadron is being disbanded and you are flying home. But remember you will have only the uniform you are wearing and you will turn in all of your uniforms and be issued new ones in the states. Also, you can only carry with you your personal shaving kit and toiletries, etc. No GI barracks bags! No souvenirs." Strict orders!

The news that I was flying home was about the best news I could have received because ever since I had crossed the North Atlantic to France on a crowded troop ship, in mid-winter with 40 foot waves, I had dreaded the thought of crossing it again. The news that I was flying home seemed to be an answer to prayer. But I was cautiously optimistic. I really hated to get rid of my "liberated souvenirs" that included a set of perfectly matched 18th century flintlock dueling pistols in a velvet case in perfect condition. But I held on to some German military medals, a couple of watches, and few other things that I could carry in my shaving kit.

## SO LONG, BOB & JACK

One of my best buddies in the 32nd TCS was Sgt. Leroy McNair from Cushing, Oklahoma. His mother was a full blooded Cherokee Indian and his dad was a full blooded Irishman. Leroy was proud of his Indian blood and his Irish blood. We became very close and talked a lot about our families and what we were going to do when we were discharged. We both intended to continue our education. A few weeks before I left Buschlag, Leroy received a letter that had been two weeks getting to him. The letter said his father had died suddenly of a heart attack. The news was absolutely devastating to Leroy. He and his father were very close and had made plans to ranch together in Oklahoma after the war.

After getting the news his father had died, Leroy brought the letter to me to read. He began sharing some of his childhood experiences with his father and Indian grandfather. We sat up all night talking and it seemed to help ease the pain and grief he had built up inside. Leroy was not scheduled to be rotated back to the states for another year and when I left him, he said he was now going to make a career of the Army.

Before Bob Hassinger and I left Buschlag, Leroy threw a goodbye party for us. There was a large cake with "So Long Bob & Jack" on the top. It was quite a gala affair; we were considered "special" because we were going to fly home. I never knew what happened to Leroy McNair, the Irish-Indian from Cushing, Oklahoma, who had become such a close friend. But I was excited about the prospect of flying home to my Kentucky hills.

When I arrived on the air base I joined the 25 or 30 lucky GIs who were flying home for Christmas, and everything seemed to be falling into place. (That was two weeks before Thanksgiving.) We were told we were flying back on the next military transport plane cleared to return to the states. After everyone was assigned to one barracks, we were told we were on "alert" for the next flight cleared to cross the

Bob Hassinger and Jack Ellis waiting to fly home.

Atlantic. We could not leave the base and we even had to sign out when we went to the PX (Post Exchange). Our morale could not have been any higher and we were a happy bunch of GIs.

## HURRY UP AND WAIT

We waited patiently as a week passed. Then two weeks, and no plane to take us home. We were called in and told no planes were being cleared to fly back yet. We were given the opportunity to vote on going back by surface transportation. But we voted to continue to wait on the military transport plane. Three weeks passed and we voted again to wait on the mysterious plane to be cleared for take off. Thanksgiving passed and we were still in Germany.

After four weeks of waiting on "alert" status we were told we could still wait on the next flight home or we could vote to go home on the next troop ship home. We were assured we would be given first priority on the next troop ship and still be home for Christmas. With that assurance we voted to go via surface craft. However, there was another military snafu! Although I did not know it at the time, the first planeload of soldiers (we had not been the first) that took off back to the states had crashed at Gander, Newfoundland. There were no survivors! That was why the military was so cautious about clearing another flight. That was another time God was taking care of me and I didn't realize it.

Stripped of his "liberated" souvenirs and waiting patiently to fly home from Germany, 1946.

## FROM FLYING HOME TO CROWDED TROOP SHIP

We were finally packed on a crowded troop train at Frankfurt and sent to the German port of Bremerhaven on the North Sea. When we arrived we told the people processing us that we had first priority. They laughed at us. (snafu!) We were there a week screaming we had priority and were told "We never heard of you." But I recall while at Bremerhaven the ban against GIs marrying German girls had been lifted. The next day the *Stars & Stripes* headlines announced that 5,000 GIs in Germany went AWOL (absent without leave), returning to marry German girls. But I was not one of them and boarded a troop ship on December 14 which I recall as one of the coldest days I ever experienced. As we lined up for hours to board the ship, the wind coming off of the

Ban against GIs marrying German girls lifted.

North Sea was absolutely bone chilling. It was a good thing we were reissued GI overcoats after we voted to come home on a troop ship. It was another time that heavy, bulky GI overcoat saved me.

As the ship steamed westward toward New York, we were able to exchange our German occupation currency, which we called "funny money," for good old American "greenbacks." Believe me, George Washington and Abraham Lincoln never looked so good. But I soon lost most of them in a poker game. Broke and almost back in the states, I sold my Rolex Oyster Perpetual watch to another GI who had tried to buy it from me ever since we embarked. I sold it to him for $300, which I thought was a pretty good profit from the $40 I paid for the watch.

The voyage home was fairly uneventful except for a few forty foot waves, whales, and several silent icebergs in the mist. As I

From flying home to crowded troop ship home, a big disappointment.

remembered the fate of the "unsinkable Titanic" I was thankful for the new technology called radar. During the voyage home I became friends with another GI, (not from my squadron) whom I had never seen before. He was carrying two barracks bags with him wherever he went. He finally opened them up so I could see they were both full of "liberated souvenirs, watches, rings, diamonds, and jewelry." I said, "How are you ever going to get those things off the ship and out the gate?" He said he had a plan to get them home to Pennsylvania.

## MISSING CHRISTMAS AGAIN

As the sun rose on December 24, we entered New York Harbor with the beautiful Statue of Liberty in full view. It was good to be back in the states but I wasn't home yet. Before leaving the ship we

Kroenburg Castle near Bad Homburg where $8,000,000 in jewels and gold were "liberated."

had to sign a declaration saying we had no illegal contraband. The GI with his two bags full of liberated contraband got off the ship without any problem. He and I boarded a troop train directly off the ship and it took us to the Fort Dix, New Jersey Separation Center. Since it was Christmas Eve we were processed immediately and given a three-day pass before being discharged the next week.

After arriving at Fort Dix, my new GI friend with the two barracks bags full of liberated loot waited until dark and carried the bags to the isolated back part of the base and tossed them over the back fence. He then returned to exit the front gate with his three-day pass on his way home to Pennsylvania. As we went out the gate everyone was stopped and all contraband and liberated articles were confiscated. Of course he was smart enough to not have his, and once outside the gate, he got off the bus at the first stop, and went back to the darkness to where he had hidden his "liberated" loot-filled barracks bags. After retrieving them, he boarded the next bus and made it home to Pennsylvania with everything he had. After his three day pass was over he returned to Ft. Dix, was discharged, and returned home again to his liberated loot.

With my three-day pass for December 25, 26, and 27, there was no way I could get home to Kentucky and back to be discharged the following week. Therefore several of us went into New York City to spend Christmas in the "Big Apple." We stayed at a YMCA and took in the sights. But Christmas Day was very lonely, especially after calling home and no one answered. (No answering machines either.) That Christmas in New York City, it struck me that there was very little English spoken on the streets, buses, and subways. It seemed ironic to me that I had heard more English spoken on the streets of Frankfurt, Germany than in New York City in 1946.

## HOME FOR NEW YEAR

As I remembered my one-year re-enlistment was up on December 23, and I thought I would be home for Christmas, but I did not make it home b-ecause of yet another snafu. After spending the three-day pass in New York City, I returned on December 27, and by December 30 was processed, separated, and handed that piece of paper (Discharge). That, along with back pay, overseas pay, and travel pay, I thought I was filthy rich. Also, I was paid for 30 days of accrued leave and my discharge post dated to January 23, 1947. As I came out the gate I

This flight jacket with squadron and my name confiscated by MPs.

had packed my leather fleece-lined flying jacket into my duffle bag. Just when I thought I was home free, the MPs swooped down on the

Happy GIs proudly display their discharges.

bus and confiscated the jacket. I wasn't going to argue with them. I'm sure they kept the jacket themselves, even though it had my name, and 32nd T.C.S. squadron sign on it.

For the third consecutive year I missed Christmas at home with my family. But I did arrive in Morehead on New Year's Eve, 1946. That meant I would not be

A WWII Veteran home at last and still a teenager, 1946.

home for Christmas until 1947. That was the song I sang in 1944, before entering active duty in the A.S.T.P in 1944. As I stepped off the train and was finally home, I breathed a prayer of thanksgiving. When I walked into our home, Mother and Dad were shocked and happy to see me. They did not even know I was in the states. After two-and-one-half years in WWII, and the Army of occupation in Germany, I was still a teenager and would not turn 20 for another 10 days. My military service was over and I was a civilian again. I had been the youngest man in the 32nd Troop Carrier Squadron, and 50 years later when I attended a squadron reunion in New York City, I was still the youngest man in the squadron. At that reunion I was voted squadron archivist and all the archives for the 32nd Troop Carrier Squadron were turned over to me. Squadron members had been collecting those documents for many years. Those records included the complete history of the 32nd Troop Carrier Squadron during its existence from 1942 until it was deactivated in 1946. I had been one of the last men in the squadron when it was deactivated.

After receiving all of the Squadron archives, I spent months organizing them for greater accessibility. They were then shipped to the Dover Air Force Base in Delaware for permanent storage as voted by members of the late great 32nd Troop Carrier Squadron.

2004 Reunion of surviving members of the 32nd T.C.S. met in Washington, D.C. Each member presented with WWII Victory Medal. J. Ellis (F) second from left, elected Squadron Archivist.

## COMMANDING OFFICERS
## 32ND TROOP CARRIER SQUADRON, 1942 - 1945

| | |
|---|---|
| March 9, 1942 | Lt. Larabee C. Lillie |
| May 14, 1942 | Lt. John W. Blakeslee |
| June 15, 1942 | Lt. Paul W. Trenkenshuh |
| July 6, 1942 | Lt. Hollis Tara |
| July 10, 1942 | Lt. Robert I. Flanigan |
| November 10, 1942 | Capt. Sterling T. Love |
| May 25, 1943 | Capt. William R. Bomar |
| July 12, 1943 | Capt. Richard B. Ott (Acting C.O.) |
| July 23, 1943 | Capt. Charles Lewelling |
| May 30, 1944 | Lt. Col. Halac G. Wilson |
| April 1945 | Major Shirley B. Thompson |
| November 2, 1945 - 1946 | Major Robert H. Riemensnider |

## OPERATIONS OFFICERS
## 32ND TROOP CARRIER SQUADRON, 1942 - 1945

| | |
|---|---|
| July - August 1942 | Lt. Whitman R. Peek |
| September - December 1942 | Lt. Hollis B. Tara |
| January - February 1943 | Lt. Robert I. Flanigan |
| March - May 1943 | Capt. George E. Falkner |
| May - June 1943 | 1st Lt. Shirley B. Thompson |
| July - November 1943 | 1st Lt. Stephen Oliphant |
| November 1943 - September 1944 | |
| | 1st Lt. Willard Webb |
| September 1944 - March 1945 | Capt. Shirley B. Thompson |
| April 1945 | Capt. Sidney Weitzman |
| May 1945 | Capt. Harley E. Shotliff |
| June - July 1945 | Capt. Sherman F. Schroder |
| August - September 1945 | Capt. Harley E. Shotliff |
| September 15, 1945 | Capt. Emil R. Schmidt |

The original "Ruptured Duck" was a cloth insignia depicting an eagle inside a wreath. It was worn on uniforms above the right breast pocket by World War II servicemen and women. It was issued to service personnel who were about to leave the military with an honorable discharge. It also allowed them to continue to wear their uniforms for up to 30 days after they were discharged since there was a clothing shortage at that time. This showed military police they were in transit and not absent without leave. As more and more men were discharged, a small gold lapel button depicting an eagle inside a wreath replaced the cloth patch. The servicemen thought the eagle looked more like a duck, and because it meant they were going home, the popular saying was, "They took off like a Ruptured Duck"... hence the nickname. (*See color version on book cover.*)

## 32ND TROOP PARTIAL ROSTER

Edward S. Ash (P)

Paul Beene (AD)

Richard N. Bell (AD) (X)

Harry Bonnes (N) (X) (A)

Milton R. Brougham (MC) (X)

Walter W. Brown (N) (X) (A)

Robert C. Browning (AD)

James R. Buckwater

Harold F. Burkins (MC)

Robert Burns (P) (A)

Isadore Caplan (N) (A)

Kenneth G. Carter (P)

Vincent R. Chiodo (P) (X) (A)

Richard C. Clause (P) (X) (A)

Harvey Cohen (N) (A)

Allan Denson (AD) (A)

John R. Driver (P) (A)

Jack E. Dycus (P)

William Elston (P) (A)

George H. Erickson (P) (A)

Jack D. Ellis (AD) (A)

Willard J. Eyer (P)

George E. Falkner (P) (X) (A)

Kenneth E. Ferguson

Walter O. Finley (P)

Herschel D. Flynn (P)

John A. Forsyth (P)

Paul C. Francke (P) (A)

James Freeborn (P)

Quentin L. Freeman (P)

Richard M. Freeman (P) (A)

James A. Fuller, Jr. (P) (A)

Charles R. Galloway (P)

William S. Garwood (P) (A)

Richard C. Gesell (P)

John M. Gibson (AD) (X)

Ralph B. Goodson, Jr. (P)

Arnljot J. Granheim (P) (A)

John C. Green (AD)

Aurel Frank Grgasivich (P)

Arthur Gruel (P)

Edward S. Guerry (P) (A)

Myron L. Guisewite (P) (A)

Lon C. Gunnoe, Jr. (P)

Patrick J. Halloran (P)

Richard C. Hardin (P) (A)

James E. Harriss (P)

William M. Henry (P) (A)

Edmund Heyman (P)

Harmon Hightower (P) (A)

Norval E. Humphrey (N)

William Husztek (N) (A)

Ted Jameson

Wallace R. Johnson (P)

William C. Jones (P)

Leonard Keller (P)

Lamar Kemp (P)

David Klarer (N) (A)

Saul S. "Sonny" Knazick (P)

Zander Koop (P) (A)

Edgar F. Kotes (P)

Jacob Kratt, Jr. (P) (A)

Dwight E. Kroesch (P) (X) (A)

*(we have lost Junior's address*—**HELP**)

Richard Lease, Jr. (P)

Charles Lewelling (P) (A)

Frederick S. Lieber, Jr. (P) (A)

William F. Linn (AD) (X) (A)

Elbert Lipman (N)

Andrew Lisak (P)

Lloyd Lockman (P)

Rogert N. Lund

Bernard F. Lynam (P)

William P. Maloney (N)

Arthur Mancuso (P) (A)

James Mattingly (P)

James Maxwell (P)

John G. McDonald (P) (X)

James T. McMurphy (X)

Aubrey C. Mendle (AD)

Ralph E. Miller (P)

Walter L. Moore (P) (A)

Edward T. Mulhern (P)

Melvin Noecker (P) (A)

Lewis M. Oatley (P)

Stephen Oliphant (P)

This campaign ribbon was awarded to those in military service who, like myself, served in the European Theater during World War II. There were two major theaters of operation during World War II, the European and the Pacific. The European conflict included service in Europe as well as Africa and the Middle East. The green, white, and red stripes on the left of the ribbon represent Italy. The white, black, and white stripes on the right of the ribbon represent Germany. The red, white, and blue stripes in the middle represent the United States. The stars represent the number of major operatives undertaken in the European theater; a bronze star represents one, and a silver star represents five. There were 16 major conflicts in Europe, Africa, and the Middle East during WWII. (*See color version on book cover.*)

# Bibliography of Sources

Although this book is autobiographical, several sources were used to confirm dates, places and events.

## ARCHIVES

32nd Troop Carrier Squadron Archives, 1942 - 1946. This writer was a member of the 32nd T.C.S. when it was decommissioned in Germany, October 30, 1946. Members of the 32nd T.C.S. collected documents for over 50 years and at our reunion in 2000, I was elected Squadron Archivist. My responsibility was to select, preserve, organize, and forward this collection to Dover Air Force Museum in Dover, Delaware. It was a "labor of love," and those "sacred" documents were forwarded to Dover in 2005. (Many duplicate documents, photos, and orders I retained, others I copied and kept in my collection.)

Kentucky Department for Library and Archives, Frankfort, Kentucky.

Morehead State University's Camden-Carroll Library.

## BOOKS

Ellis, Jack D. *Patriots and Heroes: Eastern Kentucky Soldiers of WWII.* Ashland, KY: Jesse Stuart Foundation, 2003.

*History of the Second World War.* Time-Life Books: New York, 1989.

*Holy Bible:* King James Edition.

Van Reken, Donald L. *The 32nd Troop Carrier Squadron, 1942 - 1945.* Holland, 1989.

West, Rodney T. *Honolulu Prepares for Japan's Attack: Establishment of Results of the Oahu Civilian Disaster Preparedness Programs, May 15, 1940 to December 7, 1941.* Disaster, 2003.

## DOCUMENT
Rowan County Board of Education Records, 1940 - 1945.

## MAGAZINE
*Yank: The Army Weekly,* 1945 - 1946.

## NEWSPAPERS
*Breck Eaglet,* 1940 - 1945.

*Keesler Field Times,* 1942 - 1944.

*Morehead Independent,* 1938 - 1945.

*Mountain Cruiser,* 1942 - 1944.

*Rowan County News,* 1933 - 1946.

*Trail Blazer,* 1942 - 1944.

## UNPUBLISHED DOCUMENT
Curtis, Tony. *Morehead, Kentucky: A Small Town Goes to War.* 2007.

# Jack D. Ellis

Dr. Jack D. Ellis was born in Morehead, Kentucky, January 10, 1927. He attended Breckinridge Training School and graduated from Morehead High School. He holds degrees from Morehead State University, Vanderbilt University, and the University of Southern Mississippi. He is a retired Director of Libraries and Chair of the Department of Library Science and Instructional Media at Morehead State University. He also served as Supervisor of Library Media Services for Pinellas County (Florida) Schools as well as a Media Consultant for Cornett Educational Media, a Division of Esquire, Inc.

Dr. Ellis was a member of the Florida Library and Archives Commission for eight years, having been appointed by two governors, as well as a member of the Kentucky Library and Archives Commission for 36 years, being appointed by seven governors.

Dr. Ellis is the author of four other books published by the Jesse Stuart Foundation. He also wrote a weekly column in the *Morehead News*: "Kentucky Memories: People and Places" (1997 – 2009).

A United Methodist Pastor, Dr. Ellis served six United Methodist churches in four counties in Eastern Kentucky. He also served as a volunteer chaplain at St. Claire Regional Hospital in Morehead, Kentucky.

He was a member of the 32nd Troop Carrier Squadron, Army Air Corps, in Europe during World War II. Dr. Ellis is also one of the original members of the Rowan County Veterans Committee, established in 1998, and is a life member of the Veterans of Foreign Wars.

On October 29, 2010, Dr. Ellis received Morehead State University's Founders Day Award for University Service.

Dr. Ellis is married to Janis Caudill Ellis and they have four children: Jackie, John, Jeff, and Jean; and 11 grandchildren.

# Other Books by Jack D. Ellis

*Morehead Memories: True Stories from Eastern Kentucky*, 2001; 592-page hardback with photographic illustrations and a full-color dust jacket. Out of print, but originally priced at $35.

*Patriots and Heroes: Eastern Kentucky Soldiers of WWII*, 2003; 414-page hard back book with full-color dust jacket, $35.

*Alpha M. Hutchinson: The Biography of A Man And His Community*, 2003; 160-page soft cover book with photographic illustrations and full-color cover, $15.

*Kentucky Memoires: Reflections of Rowan County*, 1856 - 2006, 2005; 448-page hardback book with photographic illustrations and full-color dust jacket, $35.

All of these books, except *Morehead Memories*, are in print and may be ordered from the Jesse Stuart Foundation. Please add $6 for shipping and send your check to the Jesse Stuart Foundation, 1645 Winchester Avenue, Ashland, KY 41101.

A World War II service flag with a blue star was hung in the homes of those who had family members in military service. (*See color version on book cover.*) A flag with a gold star meant a family member had died in military service.

# About the Publisher

Jesse Stuart Foundation

The Jesse Stuart Foundation (JSF) is devoted to preserving the human and literary legacy of Jesse Stuart and other Kentucky and Appalachian writers. The Foundation controls the rights to Stuart's published and unpublished literary works. The JSF has reprinted many of Stuart's out-of-print books along with other books that focus on Kentucky and Appalachia, and it has evolved into a significant regional press and bookseller.

The Foundation also promotes a number of cultural and educational programs. We encourage the study of Jesse Stuart's works and related regional materials.

Our primary purpose is to produce books which supplement the educational system at all levels. We have thousands of books in stock and we want to make them accessible to teachers and librarians, as well as general readers. We also promote Stuart's legacy through videotapes, dramas, readings, and other presentations for school and civic groups, and an annual Jesse Stuart Weekend at Greenbo Lake State Resort Park.

We are proud that Jesse Stuart's books are a guideline to

the solid values of America's past. Today, we are so caught up in teaching children to read that the process has obscured its higher purpose. Children require more than literacy. They need to learn, from reading, the unalterable principles of right and wrong.

That is why Stuart's books are so important. They allow educators and parents to make reading fun for children while teaching solid values at the same time. In a world that is rapidly losing perspective, the JSF is working to educate tomorrow's adults for responsible citizenship.